PORTRAIT
OF A
VERTICAL MAN

Maurice Nicoll

PORTRAIT OF A VERTICAL MAN

An appreciation of Doctor Maurice Nicoll and his work

SAMUEL COPLEY

SWAYNE PUBLICATIONS
46 GREAT RUSSELL STREET
LONDON WC1

First published in Great Britain in 1989
by Swayne Publications
46 Great Russell Street
London
WC1B 3PE

British Library Cataloguing in Publication Data

Copley, Samuel
Portrait of a vertical man: an appreciation of
Doctor Maurice Nicoll and his work.
1. English philosophy. Nicoll, Maurice, 1884-1953
I. Title
192

ISBN 0-9514414-0-X

Typeset by Litho Link Ltd., Welshpool, Powys, Wales.
Printed and bound by Camelot Press Ltd., Southampton.

ACKNOWLEDGEMENT

My heartfelt thanks are due to:–

Peter Gloster who first introduced me to Dr Nicoll and "The Work" and lately pressed me gently into writing this book.

Hester Lord for her invaluable contribution included in Chapter V.

Many other of my contemporary fellow students of Dr Nicoll (including my wife) for encouragement, support and material.

Jeffrey Somers and Kenneth Page for their unstinted material help and advice in preparing this book for publication.

None of them are responsible for mistakes, omissions or opinions which are mine alone.

ALSO to members of The Gurdjieff Society who have listened to and shared my questions, deliberately not answering them but helping me to widen and focus them so that I may go on searching and, perhaps, finding one day that there is just one big, fundamental question.

CONTENTS

Introduction

Dr. Maurice Nicoll represents one of the most important influences in my life and, I am sure, in the lives of many others.

A biography has been written by the late Mrs. Beryl Pogson who was not only his secretary in the later years of his life but also conducted extensive research on his behalf into various matters that engaged his wide ranging interest. Her book "Maurice Nicoll" (Vincent Stuart Ltd. 1961) was written in her own inimitable style with a charming naivety and a great warmth of affection. It gives a lively impression of the man. Nevertheless a biography is primarily a chronicle of the events of a life from birth to death along the dimension of passing time. Greatly daring, this book attempts to paint a word-picture of the whole man so as to include another, qualitative, dimensions with particular regard to his stature in understanding and his attitude to life. A difficult and delicate task; perhaps impossible of fulfilment. To this end I have chosen some of the main developments in his life and tried to show how, whilst always acknowledging and being grateful to his teachers and sources of inspiration, he found his own feet and centre of gravity in each adventure and thenceforth spoke and wrote from his own authority.

I use the phrase "word-picture" because Maurice Nicoll himself considered that meaning comes first and words are used for its expression in much the same way that pigment and brushes are used by an artist to express something that ultimately is beyond expression. He added that a writer, by putting himself under the extra laws of poetry, could express more subtle meaning than the prose writer. By the words "Fifth Dimension" I mean to convey something and analogous to the word "Eternity" as used by Eckhardt, Boehme and others who see this state as an extension of experience in a dimension incomprehensible to time-based and sense-based thinking. Passing time extended endlessly in its own dimension would never produce a moment of eternity whereas an experience of "here and now" might afford a glimpse of an entirely new world.

Dr. Nicoll's artistry in extracting and refining meaning from all aspects of life was considerable. He defined Hell as "absolute meaninglessness" and taught that without meaning a man may die psychologically although physically he may continue to exist. This artistry included a capacity to awaken in others an interest in developing their own innate but often unrecognised potentiality for similar artistic endeavour.

CHAPTER 1

Religion

Christianity really mattered to Maurice Nicoll. His interest in religion was not merely scholastic but also deeply emotional. Yet his early contact with the religion dispensed from the pulpit in his early life and by his schoolmasters was such that he might well have become an atheist.

He was born in a manse at Lumsden in Scotland where his father was a minister of the local Free Church. William Robertson Nicoll (later Sir William) was not only a pillar of the Church but became a considerable figure in the literary world. He seems to have been a dominating character for whom his son had admiration and respect, but also a measure of awe amounting to fear on occasions in his younger years. The son found his father and his associates overpowering. "We were brought up more in fear of the devil than in the love of God" he told us much later. The report of a conversation in March 1948 gives a picture of his Scottish environment. "My father was ruined by Presbyterianism. That's why he left the manse and came to England. He looked like a poet. He was a poet. His two sisters wrote quite good poetry and my Uncle Harry wrote that book about Victorian literature which, I believe, you can still find in libraries. They all died quite young of T.B. It was because of a very poor diet of Scots oatmeal and nothing else. My grandfather did not die of T.B. He was a very spare man. He collected 12,000 books out of his income of £200 per year. So you can see there was not much left for food. He always preached 'The Mercy of God' and 'The Holy Ghost', the elders disapproving of course".

This is confirmed by T. H. Darlow in his book "William Robertson Nicoll. His Life and Letters" published by Hodder & Stoughton in 1925. Here the number of books in the library is said to be 17,000 and the income never up to £200 but nearer £100 per annum. The books included over 100 different editions of the Greek New Testament. The household lived mainly on vegetables, porridge and dairy produce. There was a cow. W. R. Nicoll as a boy seldom tasted beef until he went to lodge in Aberdeen. He confessed in later years, "I always feel that I was defrauded of my youth—there was little sunshine in it—far too little".

With this dour background it is scarcely surprising that Maurice Nicoll had a jaundiced opinion of religion in his native country.

In one of his "Psychological Commentaries on the Teaching of G. I. Gurdjieff and P. D. Ouspensky" (Vol. 1, p.8), Dr. Nicoll relates an early experience of breaking through the barrier of religion "as taught" into his own understanding.

"I was brought up in regard to religious ideas with the sense that only the conviction of sin was important. Everything was sin briefly speaking. In consequence religion was a very gloomy business and personally I loathed it. Morality was only sexual morality, virtue was continence and so on and, in general, sin and the feeling of being a sinner was the main idea of religion. I never understood anything else in regard to religion as a boy and so I was either afraid, worried or hated the whole thing. I began to stammer badly. I listened to the Scriptures, mostly drawn from the Old Testament, which always sounded horrible. God was a violent, jealous, evil and accusing person and so on. And when I heard the New Testament I could not understand what the parables meant and no one seemed to care what they meant. But once, in a Greek New Testament class, on Sundays taken by the Headmaster, I dared to ask, in spite of my stammer, what some parable meant. The answer was so confused that I actually experienced my first moment of consciousness—that is, I suddenly realised that no one knew anything. This is a definite experience of Self Remembering, the second being the sudden realisation that no one knew what I was thinking—and from that moment I began to think for myself, or rather knew that I could. As you know, all real moments of Self Remembering stand out for ever in one's inner life. One's real life is not outer events, but inner states. I remember so clearly this classroom, the high windows constructed so that we could not see out of them, the desks, the platform on which the Headmaster sat, his scholarly, thin face, his nervous habit of twitching his mouth and jerking his hands, and suddenly the inner revelation of knowing that he knew nothing—nothing, that is, of anything that really mattered. This was my first liberation from the power of external life. From that time I knew for certain—and that always means by inner, individual authentic perception, which is the only source of real knowledge—that all my loathing of religion as it was taught me was right."

The expression "Self Remembering" as used in this passage has a special significance in the Gurdjieff teaching, on which Dr. Nicoll is commenting in these volumes. It means a higher or more objective state of consciousness than that in which we spend our so-called waking hours and which Gurdjieff calls "Sleep". This should be distinguished from sleep in bed which is a biological necessity. Our sleep in the sense implied by Gurdjieff is characterised day-dreams, uncontrolled imagination, suggestion from many quarters and general subjectivity to external influences.

In a state of Self Remembering a man finds himself in a strangely different relationship to his environment and to time. He has a different feeling of "I". He is present in the moment and receives both external and internal impressions on new, sensitive and uncluttered surfaces. A question arises, "Who am I?". Wonder replaces knowing. Such an experience usually remains only for a moment before "Sleep" reigns again. It can exist on different levels, but even though it may be forgotten in passing time, something is recorded somewhere of the taste of a new way of being.

"Self Remembering", when used as a verb, denotes the deliberate effort to rediscover this state, to uncover, to remember. This is no effort of muscle or of intellect. It is for "Man Asleep", a new kind of effort, an un-natural effort. This is one aspect of the Work. To awaken and to remember is possible for man. It is his birthright and in striving for this possibility lies true evolution. This potentiality distinguishes man from other vertebrates.

On page 1765 of volume V of the same Commentaries there appears, "Sitting in Church as a boy, and looking around the congregation, I used to think that I did not really want to go Heaven with all these worthy people".

Many years later at Great Amwell we were sitting outside the pub which was adjacent to the Church watching the congregation emerge when Dr. Nicoll remarked, "Look at those horrible 'good' faces".

All this proceeded from the mind that also produced the books, "The Mark", "Living Time" and "The New Man". Of "The

New Man" Diogenes* reviewing for "Time and Tide" wrote "Of all the books that I have read on the teaching of Jesus I have read none more valuable than this". Of "The Mark" he wrote, "Once in a thousand books we come across one which sets the mind soaring and which, we know instinctively as we read, will possess significance not just for the moment, but for all our lives. This is such a book." These are extracts from long and enthusiastic reviews.

So notwithstanding his early loathing for religion "as taught" Christianity found a place in Nicoll's being. He did not claim to be a Christian for, he said, "a Christian is one born of the spirit".

It is very tempting to quote at length from these remarkable books which, for so many, have restored Christianity to a vibrant meaningful teaching; but it would be far more profitable for readers to go directly to the books themselves.

These Gospel Commentaries run a parallel course with the "Psychological Commentaries on the Teaching of G. I. Gurdjieff and P. D. Ouspensky". There is no confusion, but they complement one another in an enlightening manner. They also combine with his knowledge of psychiatry. For instance the commandment "Judge not that ye be not judged" should, according to Nicoll, be a basic principle in every school of psychotherapy, for exactly as you appoint yourself judge of another's sins and shortcomings, so do you forge bars for your own psychological cage. If Jesus could say to the women taken in adultery, "Neither do I condemn thee", how much more should both patients and doctors allow living-space to their fellow beings, not from a spurious equanimity but from a genuine conviction that "I really do not know". Perhaps "There, but for the grace of God, am I".

There were frequent references to John the Baptist preaching "metanoia" which is poorly translated in the Bible as meaning "repentance". In fact, the Greek word is a combination of "meta" and "nous" indicating a transformation of mind; a transformation as complete as the "metamorphosis" or change of form, from an egg to a caterpillar, to a pupa, to a butterfly. We were told that

*The true identity of "Diogenes" was kept a closely guarded secret by "Time and Tide". Rumour has it that he was W. J. Brown who, apart from being the independent Member of Parliament for Rugby was also secretary of the Civil Service Clerical Union and the writer of weekly articles for the *Evening Standard*. The latter were sufficiently entertaining to divert my allegiance from the *Evening News* at that time, although I then knew nothing of his other activity, if indeed the rumour was accurate.

whereas the metamorphosis of a butterfly is manifest in passing time, under the laws of nature, metanoia takes place "Now" in a moment of eternity and is not subject to nature, but to the conscious effort of a human being to come under a different order of laws. As a result the "Kingdom" is at hand here and now, not in future time nor necessarily after physical death. Jacob Boehme points out that Christ, speaking of his sheep when they recognise him, says "I *give* them eternal life" in the present tense. Now Man's possible evolution lies in this dimension of Eternity, whereas natural, Darwinian, evolution lies in time.

In relation to "Change of Mind" or "Thinking in a new way", Ouspensky writes in "The New Model of the Universe" of his experimental mysticism under drugs and of ". . . a vividly expressed new state in which he understood all he wished to understand", and of a note he had made to remind him of what he had to do to regain this understanding next morning. It read "Think in new categories". Metanoia?

Dr. Nicoll, however, preferred to widen the concept of "change of mind" beyond that of only the mental mind so as to include the emotional mind and the instinctive mind of the body so that it affected the whole of man's being. He seemed to be at one with those gnostics who held that man's contact with God was potentially direct and not exclusively through the medium of a particular church. In fact man is a microcosmos within a macrocosmos and has god-like principles within him, but unrealised; man made in the image of God. These are principles running like warp threads through the whole fabric of the Universe from Heaven to Hell, as it were, while the weft threads of time run across the fabric carrying the history of events experienced at different levels in the dimension of time.

In my younger days, after some nudging from Dr. Nicoll, I read Plato's "Republic" from the point of view that it was a psychological study as well as a political one. It was fascinating to conjecture what in my being corresponded to the ideal state when kings shall be philosophers and philosophers shall be kings, and then to aristocracy, timocracy, oligarchy, democracy (many "I"s) to the tyrant or dictator who first brings some benefits to the State, but having put the cup of power to his lips cannot take it away and forms his infamous bodyguard and liquidates his rivals. Perhaps, also, my ordinary perception was as that of the cave dwellers who took two-dimensional shadows as solid reality.

In spite of his rebellion against established views, Dr. Nicoll was no iconoclast. He did not break other men's idols nor kick away their crutches. He had a deep respect for truth and goodness wherever it was found. He spoke of his experiences during the first world war and of his respect for the discipline and devotion shown by Roman Catholic priests who would make their way to the thickest of the fighting to administer last rites to dying soldiers. The men died the better and the happier for these services. Something beyond logical explanation took place and only a spiritually "dead" man would deny it. Perhaps it was the simple humility and "not knowing" of the priests in the horrific conditions of war together with their courage that wrought minor miracles.

A constantly recurring theme ran through Maurice Nicoll's talks and writing on both religion and psychology. This was the inadequacy of logical and sense-based thinking to cope with spiritual and psychological truths. Such thinking was not inappropriate for dealing with material things on their own level, but we tended to be glued to this level of thinking even when dealing with finer meaning to which it could not possibly apply. Symbolically the exodus of the Israelites from Egypt was a journey from a land of sense-based, time-bound truth towards a state of higher spiritual truth, a promised land. The Israelites were constantly back-sliding, making a Golden Calf, other graven images and worshipping them. At one point they fell so far away that they had to be provided with ten commandments engraved in stone, or hard, literal truth. "Thou shalt" and "Thou shalt not". Elsewhere Dr. Nicoll interprets stone as literal truth, water as a more fluid psychological truth and wine as spiritual truth.

Christ's commandment to love God and love thy neighbour could only be understood on a spiritual level where it superseded all other commandments. Dr. Nicoll insisted that where the Greek word "agape" is used in the Gospels it means a cosmic love, a radiation under whose influence we may sometimes be privileged to find ourselves. To talk of "making" love was blasphemy.

Reverting to the Old Testament, I remember a talk about the manna miraculously given to the Israelites in the desert (Exodus 16). Manna signified meaning which was said to be the true food of the Spirit and deprived of which a man will die. (In some ways "meaning" in this context is analogous to the "food of impressions" which, as we shall see later is the most important of three foods, ordinary food, air, and impressions, which man is given according to the teaching of Gurdjieff.) An important condition was attached to the gift of manna. It was not to be kept for the following day, unless that day happened to be the Sabbath. "Every man had a measure according to his eating" and if this rule was disregarded the conserved manna would breed worms and would stink.

In Cruden's Concordance there is a note that "manna" means "what is this?". The Shorter Oxford English Dictionary says that the word is traditionally derived from the Aramaic "Man hu?" "What is it?" From this we may assume that the food was previously unknown and therefore new to the Israelites. Likewise meaning needs to be new every day from the impressions of the day; even more strictly, new or fresh for each moment of "Now".

Not unrelated is a comment Dr. Nicoll made about nostalgia of a certain kind and home-sickness which he called the disease of looking backwards and looking into old dustbins for food. From his war experience he saw it as a definite disease which, in a man, may indicate immaturity. "He looks for Mummy".

In the Commentaries (vol.3, p.1116) he writes ". . . meaning is the most important thing for we live by meaning. We have to separate the old worn-out meaning to let in new meaning. Otherwise we die." It may be that the story of Lot's wife has a similar significance for she became crystallised into a pillar of salt on looking back to Sodom and Gomorrah.

To end this chapter I give an extract from a letter written to a sub-group leader in reply to questions raised by her group about the Lord's Prayer.

> ". . . try to think what it means for themselves especially with all that comes before the Lord's Prayer and especially the idea of Self Remembering that starts the prayer. i.e. Our Father in Heaven—not the parents of our sensible life. We pray that thy will be done on Earth . . . that means that a higher law may act on our being which is our earth. So we really pray from the beginning for a trial of ourselves in view of the higher levels. But you see the whole thing is so intensely emotional and so difficult to put into words, so tremendous in its brief formulations that I can't give you anything in detail at present. Tell your people that the prayer means that God's

will is not done on this earth or on the earth of ourselves and that therefore conclusions about the horribleness of our life mean nothing about the existence of God. Remember that this life has its meaning in terms of another life, as the Work teaches. This world is a trying-out ground."

(Letter dated 18.10.44)

CHAPTER 2

Medicine

"Medicine is an art, not a science".
"Older physicians had more of this mysterious quality than the newer scientific sort".

(Extracts from hand-written diaries)

Mrs. Pogson tells briefly of Maurice Nicoll's passage through school and university culminating in a "First" at Cambridge and a scholarship which he did not take up. However there is one episode in his Cambridge life not mentioned which indicates something of his independence of thought and method.

Although I never knew him to be more than passingly interested in horses, he said that he found the proximity of Cambridge to Newmarket not conducive to academic study so that, when the examinations approached, he found himself unprepared. He was not alone amongst undergraduates in this predicament. But whereas others would read through the small hours of the night with wet towels round their heads to make up the arrears, he found that he could economise in time and effort by another method. He erected a black-board in his room and, after reading relatively short but concise passages, he would close the book and give a lecture on the principle points at issue in his own words. He extracted meaning in place of simply memorising words. He would then move to another section and master that, finally connecting all section into a whole.

Next he qualified in medicine at St. Bartholomew's Hospital and after a voyage to Buenos Aires as a ship's surgeon, he went to Vienna to specialise in psychiatry in the Freudian School. I do not think that Freudian psychology had much attraction for this pupil for he moved on to Zurich and Dr. Jung. Here the relationship was warm and rewarding. Amongst other benefits received he credits Dr. Jung with having cured his stammering in two conversations, although he did not consult Dr. Jung with this end in view.

In freeing Dr. Nicoll from the psychological domination of his father, and thus from his stammering, Jung advised him to have a thought for his father. "How would you like to be your father with yourself as son?"

The fact that Dr. Jung became the godfather of the Nicolls' daughter, Jane, and that before Dr. Nicoll's marriage had been invited to stay at a cottage in Buckinghamshire which Dr. Nicoll was sharing with others as a week-end retreat, shows the warmth of their relationship. This continued after Dr. Nicoll had parted from Jung professionally and gone his own way. Dr. Nicoll always acknowledged a deep gratitude and respected Jung's views on the value of dreams as a clue to understanding a patient's problems. With his interest in symbols, archetypes and the "collective unconscious" Jung looked upwards and outwards as well as inwards and downwards for his understanding on man's psyche.

Dr. Nicoll tried to keep aloof from the Freud-Jung argument, but in his book, "Dream Psychology" published in 1917 he wrote, "Broadly speaking associations may lead in two directions. There are reductive associations which, like chemical analysis, reduce the symbol into its elementary parts. This is the Freudian method of approach. On the other hand there are constructive associations which shape and develop the symbol to fit in with the immediate life of the dreamer and so bring it to the level of contemporary experience as a living thing. This is the method used by the Zurich School under Dr. Jung." He also questioned the "wish fulfilment theories of Freud which were almost always connected with sex (p.58 ibid). On page 177 he writes "The Freudian concept of the unconscious seems only to concern itself with repressed material . . . what happens when the repressed material is liberated? Can it be said that any "unconscious" remains and, if so, what is its function?"

[Footnote on the Buckinghamshire Cottage.

In her biography of Dr. Nicoll* Mrs. Pogson refers to Dr. Jung's interest in a haunted room in this cottage. I think she must be wrong in locating it at Chorley Wood which is a long way from Aylesbury station, from which Nicoll cycled, and from Waddesdon Manor, to which the two doctors walked. Living in the district I think it more likely that the

*Maurice Nicoll. 1961 Vincent Stuart Ltd.

cottage was in the hamlet of Chearsley which is about five miles from Aylesbury and a similar distance from Waddesdon. Recently a wychert cottage collapsed in a gale at Chearsley and one wonders whether this may be the same and related to the unhappy ghost who disturbed the doctors. Wychert is a local mud, a seam of which stretches from Aylesbury to Long Crendon and of which the walls of some local buildings were formed up until the beginning of the last war.]

Dr. Nicoll's view of medicine generally tended towards what is nowadays called holistic. Whilst he did not under-value specialisation, he thought the tendency to explain everything by breaking it down into its component parts and then breaking those parts still further was inadequate unless the doctor also looked outwards towards the body in which the diseased organ was contained and then further outwards towards all surrounding conditions, including the psychological. You may be able to learn something about a little finger by studying the different types of tissue, the cells, atoms, and so on, but you do not understand a little finger until you comprehend its relation to the hand and the hand's relation to the arm, to the body and to the whole man, and then man to the whole of organic life on earth. We shall see that he applied the "constructive" principle as well as the "reductive" to all forms of scientific and philosophic enquiry.

He made a special study of shell-shock during and after the first world war and spoke of the reluctance with which its existence as a definite illness was acknowledged by medical men of the day. They tended to regard it as a moral lapse. He mentioned the case of a soldier whose hold on life was slipping when a telegram or letter arrived from his girl friend containing a message, "I love you" or something similar. His health began to improve immediately. There may have been a degree of satirical exaggeration when Dr. Nicoll said, "The doctors wanted to analyse the ink on the telegram rather than to admit that the message itself led to the recovery".

In "Dream Psychology" what is now called "Body Language" was anticipated by half a century for when a patient describes a dream, the way he recounts it may be, and probably is, of more significance than what he says. "This second language reveals itself in a great number of small ways in a language that is difficult to describe and yet is unmistakable in its meaning. It is a curious language of gestures, hesitation, change in colour, voice, tone and expression. It is a language that shines through the speech itself . . . its peculiarity is that it is understood by all human beings and, apparently, to a greater or lesser extent by animals."

For similar reasons the symbolism of a dream cannot be interpreted without taking into account the dreamer. There is no kind of Latin vocabulary, "mensa equals table", a bicycle, two round wheels and a bar in between equals a sex symbol, etc. Therefore later on, when he had abandoned psychiatry, Dr. Nicoll's pupils were not encouraged to interpret each other's dreams lest they became too intellectual, without significant all-round experience and inner version. One might call it "Clear Seeing", to avoid the connotations of the French equivalent when used by the English.

In a "Commentary" dated 20th November 1943 entitled "A Brief Talk about Dreams", we are told that only a few dreams carry significant meaning. All psychological systems based on the study of dreams are fantastic because "as soon as you begin to study your dreams they alter . . . your instrument of investigation interferes with what you are investigating . . . you strike a match to see whether there is a mouse in the room and probably the mouse disappears! "The study of dreams as a psychological approach to oneself is definitely discouraged." He goes on to say that although many ordinary dreams are caused by physical and external circumstances there are others occasionally of a different quality arising from more internal sources. "Strange dreams, sometimes very wonderfully worked out and containing some meaning that we cannot catch."

The modification of his thoughts on dreams between 1917 and 1943 is probably due to the fact that he later considers them in the light of Gurdjieff's teaching and then concludes in his own idiom, "The language of dreams is not put in the form of words. It is put in the language of imagery. It is exactly comparable to the language of parables. It is quite true that the parables are expressed by the means of words, but they indicate images. You all know that you do not dream words but, if you want to describe a dream, you have to turn to words and you soon lose its meaning. In fact you cannot express it in words save in a very poor way. Parables are the other way round. They are expressed in words, usually very simply, but they transmit imagery" . . . "we see the beginning of a universal language which is the language of Higher Emotional Centre."*

I shall describe a dream which I had many years ago and Dr. Nicoll's interpretation of its meaning.

The dreams were in two parts. In the first I was standing on the end of a girder swung from a crane on a building site. I knew that I had to jump off and when I did so I found that the height was only a matter of inches. In the second part I found myself having to serve in some way a young man who in real life had previously served me. He had been appointed first lieutenant of a small minesweeper which I commanded. He served cheerfully and well although he had some grounds for being disappointed with the appointment. This was after hostilities had ended and he had come from the relatively glamorous "Coastal Forces" and would probably have had a command of his own in a motor torpedo boat, had they not been laid up. Meanwhile there remained plenty of work in mine clearance.

In the dream I was not unhappy with the reversed rôles.

Dr. Nicoll wrote:

> "This is a good but not unusual representation of the 'Work', erecting buildings etc. with the crane above. The young man is your 'Life' self. You feel nervous because of the contrast between the young man and your 'Work' self, yet you find that you are exaggerating and have only six inches to the ground. This serving of one's life self is something far more interesting. Notice what you say and apply it to yourself of course. You are the inner man and he represents the outer man in yourself. One must labour at the 'personality' which a greater must serve. Notice here what Christ said about 'who would be first among you?'
>
> "The double aspect of the Work, making it seem nothing but paradox at first is well shown in the Gnostic hymn of Christ which he is said to have danced with his disciples and in which such phrases as, 'I would pierce and I would be pierced' occur which seem opposite and contradictory. One must rule and serve and serve and rule. One must control one's personality and submit to it, and submit to it and control it. This to and fro motion Gurdjieff showed me in a dream at The Institute very clearly by means of a rolling pin by which I had

*The Teaching on "Centres" is briefly examined on Pages 56/57.

to squeeze out a wet sponge in a to-and-fro motion. At length the sponge became a mirror and I then knew that I had objective consciousness—IF I COULD DO IT ACTUALLY.

"So the Work says similarly, 'you must become passive to yourself (Nicoll in my case) and you must make Nicoll passive'."

Where the word "Work" is used in these pages, either in inverted commas or with a capital letter, it refers to the teaching of Gurdjieff and Ouspensky in its various aspects. The following chapter deals with the relationship of Dr. Nicoll with these two men. I think that this should be made clear at this point, but it is not my intention to expound my understanding of the teaching except where it relates to my portrait of Dr. Nicoll. Interested readers are referred to the books written by P. D. Ouspensky and G. I. Gurdjieff themselves and to Nicoll's Commentaries on their teaching. These are:—

P. D. Ouspensky

"The Psychology of Man's Possible Evolution".

"In Search of the Miraculous".

G. I. Gurdjieff

"All and Everything".

"Meetings with Remarkable Men".

M. Nicoll

"Psychological Commentaries on the Teaching of Gurdjieff and Ouspensky".

These are not the only books by these authors, but they are concerned most directly with "The Work".

Returning to medicine in general, I feel that Nicoll was not happy with contemporary psychiatry. Two extracts from his verses may indicate the root of his dissatisfaction.

"Ah! Unhappy days
When everything is explained
And nothing understood."

and another,

"The feelings of boyhood
Before I committed the sin
Of naming everything
And thinking that I knew.
Years before I ate

Of the Tree of Knowledge
And pretended that I knew."

In a medical notebook dated 1921 an entry reads: "Terms should not be used in analysis. People get to talk of Narcissism, auto-eroticism, etc., glibly. Terms then come to be easy ways of expressing qualities that should be realised in other ways." This illustrates Dr. Nicoll's war on words lightly used and on jargon in particular.

I have the impression that he felt that psychologists, rather like economists, want always to explain phenomena on the level at which they become manifest and in terms of what they know already. Failing sufficient words, they invent new ones and new so-called "laws". Then they are satisfied that they know. Dr. Nicoll, on the other hand, preferred to leave enquiries open ended, particularly at the upper end where words fail. He favoured living with a question rather than finding a neat answer and closing his mind to it thenceforth. He did not quarrel with scientific explanations and causality based on passing time provided that the explainer was aware of their limitations and did not dismiss the significance of what I have previously called "warp" threads. Without precisely defining the nature and effects of lunar, planetary and stellar influences on our lives, it was undeniable that they existed. It was also undeniable that there are more things in Heaven and Earth than we are aware of in all our philosophy.

Dr. Nicoll sometimes marvelled at the mystery of mitosis in our physical development. Cells divide and multiply to fulfil a design that already exists so that eventually, and provided that man has not been playing at God with hormones, D. N. A. and R. N. A., a more or less symmetrical body emerges with life. Does not causality flow in *all* dimensions including from the *future* into the present? Perhaps the parents existed for the purpose of providing an entry into the physical world of the child. Perhaps the child *is* father of the man in this sense. Then again the cause of humanity's presence in the film of organic life on Earth does not lie in time at all but is the result of an existing Cosmic requirement from a completely other direction. One requires metanoia to encompass the possibilities of such thought.

One sometimes hears talk of the birth of a child being a "mistake" resulting from ineffective contraception or some such cause. But can anyone regard his own birth and continued existence as accidental, whatever the conditions of conception may have been? What arrogance, bereft of meaning, allows us to imagine that the arising of a human being is exclusively under our control to suit our personal convenience? War, famine, disease, storm, tempest, earthquakes and motor vehicles are put on earth to check the growth of population as well as some knowledge of contraception. Man lives in these conditions which control him rather than he controlling them. Medical knowledge is also given to mitigate some of the effects of other influences, but this is only lent and may be misused by those who ascribe knowledge to themselves. "A determined spermatazoon will find its way around a condom or through a barrage of chemicals to the ovum in spite of Marie Stopes", said Dr. Nicoll.

Again, he wondered about man's relationship with animals. If you forget about natural selection and are a little alive emotionally —or instinctively—can you not feel that a working horse or a working dog has a present vibrating relationship with its master, one that is in the design of things? Why do these animals show such a willing desire to serve and work with man? (I am thinking of border collies as a particular example). Is there no mystery in this? Perhaps to an exclusively rational mind, no, but to a simpler less sophisticated one, yes.

When my father was dying I asked Dr. Nicoll whether we should employ a more up-to-date doctor than the one who had attended him for years. The answer was an unequivocal No! The two, doctor and patient, were of much the same generation, spoke the same sort of language and understood one another. The availability of modern drugs and techniques was not important in this case. It was support and understanding that mattered.

In psychological illness the actions and inactions of parents, guardians and teachers explained only a fraction of the whole. Such explanations might give temporary relief or they may create as many problems as they solve, for finally a patient must awaken to his own position from his own effort, bear his own weight and blame no one.

I asked Dr. Nicoll whether he had practised hypnotism in his medical days. He replied, "Yes. But if I have my time again I must remember not to do it". A real psychiatrist needed to be free from jargon, clichés, fixed opinions. Every time a patient consulted him it had to be a new experience to be met with a completely open mind. He needed to be something of a "seer", i.e. a person who sees with all his senses, external and internal. A good oracle, Dr. Nicoll claimed, amongst other faculties, could "see" essential types and could determine whether candidates for marriage were complementary and essentially related, so that the resulting marriage, if not necessarily comfortable, would be potentially real and rich. The fulfilment of the potentiality would inevitably require "work" by the couple for which guidance might be given by the oracle.

As an illustration of how far Dr. Nicoll's thoughts ranged beyond the rationally accepted norm, he told me years after both my parents had died, "you can release your parents now". I asked, "you mean in my own psychology?" He replied, "More than that. In such a way that they will feel the release in their own time, as well as you". It was as important for children to release their parents as for the parents to release their children and for both to try to free the others from inner debts, judgements and grudges.

We shall see later that a similar reciprocal release is necessary between teacher and taught.

As with religion, so with medicine Dr. Nicoll dug beneath the surface to find hidden truth, not forgetting to be grateful to those who helped him on his way.

"Medicine is an art, not a science". This may be an over-simplified statement, but it makes its point.

CHAPTER 3

Gurdjieff and Ouspensky

One evening in 1921, Dr. Nicoll heard Ouspensky lecturing at the Quest Society in London. Mrs. Nicoll was in bed when he returned home where, according to Mrs. Pogson's account, he shook the bed saying, "You must come and hear Ouspensky. He is the only man who has ever answered my questions". Mrs. Nicoll told me that he walked up and down for a considerable part of the night, saying at intervals, "This is it". The impact of this meeting was enough to change the course of their lives. It resulted eventually in the relinquishing of a flourishing Harley Street consultancy and of the practice of medical psychiatry.

G. I. Gurdjieff came to London in 1922 when, amongst others of Ouspensky's pupils, the Nicolls attended his meetings. When Gurdjieff formed his Institute for the Harmonious Development of Man at Avon, near Fontainbleau in France, Dr. and Mrs. Nicoll, with their one-year old daughter, a nurse and Mrs. Nicoll's sister joined the band of pupils. They stayed there for a year although Dr. Nicoll was obliged to return to England for a time to attend to family affairs on the death of his father. There appears to have been some talk of Nicoll going to the U.S.A. in connection with Gurdjieff's work, but in any case material conditions required the return of the family to England. Here they attended Ouspensky's meetings again and Dr. Nicoll received a few patients in Harley Street for a while.

Several writers have described the unique conditions of life at The Institute and some have claimed a special relationship with Mr. Gurdjieff. It is probably true that these relationships were special for this remarkable man had the capacity to see into the inner worlds of each individual and to "create conditions" specially tailored for the needs of his inner growth—if he chose to use them. (The words "create conditions" are in inverted commas because Gurdjieff did not claim to be able to awaken men and women, but said "I can only create conditions"—those are conditions in which each may awaken himself from "sleep" if, as I say, he or she cares to use them.) However Dr. Nicoll did not suffer from the "Heir Apparent" syndrome which appears to have affected some of these writers.

On the subject of succession amongst those authorised to teach "The Work" it may be appropriate here, by way of analogy, to reproduce a talk that was given on the development of a normal human being and the places of "shock" that occur in that process: again the inverted commas around a word which has a special significance in Gurdjieff's teaching.

Shock:

(1) Soon after birth the umbilicus is cut so that thenceforth the baby breathes air from a new source, the outside world.

(2) Some weeks/months later, the baby is weaned from the breast so that more solid nourishment is received, not through the mother, but from the outside world.

(3) The child goes to school, instruction, authority and impressions issue from people other than the parents.

(4) He (or she) is pushed out of the nest to be apprenticed and to earn his own living.

(5) As an adult he starts a new family, supports them and possibly, his parents in their old age.

At each shock there is a switch from one source of nourishment to another and a requirement for self-reliance and for relinquishing earlier means of support. So also with the nourishment given by the Work. Even Gurdjieff could not spoon-feed his pupils. He could only create conditions for their own emancipation. Eventually, the Work teaches, "Life becomes your teacher". Recall what was written earlier about "Homesickness" and "Looking for Mummy". Man awakening goes rather cold and naked into an unknown environment. If he is a *man* he welcomes it even though he may be apprehensive.

With this analogy in mind I sometimes wonder about the emancipation of Ouspensky, Nicoll and Orage and whether the abrupt severance of each of them from their previous sources of nourishment was not a necessary condition for their own development and their inner authority to teach. This is my own conjecture since I do not know enough about the circumstances of the separation in each case. Ouspensky writes that "Gurdjieff went in a direction that I could not follow". Was this deliberate? Dr. Nicoll was told to go—and teach the Work. Of Orage I have no first-hand knowledge but reading Gurdjieff's book, "Life is Real only then when I am" he seems to have received the treatment that only a very worthy man could accept with such a positive attitude. In each case these men directed many faithful followers to their late teacher and started again with new groups and without recrimination.

It seems that this "shock" was necessary. For each man life had to become his teacher so that he spoke and acted from his own experience and not just by the book. They had to find their own idioms.

The word "idiom" had the same Greek root, idios, as the word "idiot". By derivation "idiotes" can mean a private person, *individual,* a common man, an ill-informed man (perhaps one who has the grace of now knowing). I mention this because when I later met a number of people who had been direct pupils of Gurdjieff, they referred to the endless toasts to their "idiots" which he required them to drink at his table. It would seem that our "idiots" are important, perhaps related to Essence* in the mind of Gurdjieff who may well have given the Greek meaning to the word far more importance than the English meaning of "fool".

Whether I am right or wrong in applying the analogy to Ouspensky, Nicoll and Orage, I was told on one occasion, that I must be free from my teacher and he free from me, as with father and son. Nicoll said that although I should be ever grateful to my teacher, perhaps love him, my meaning must come from within and from my own experience of life. Secondhand meaning and repeating other men's words was of no use in the end. The Work had to touch men and women directly. "If people take the Work only through me they will have to take it in spite of me". Here he gave a lurid description, which I shall not repeat, of the image he would project in order to shake them off his coat-tails. If they left the Work because of this it would be no great loss. They would never have profited from it, nor would the Work have profited from them.

An early pupil recalls Nicoll's remark, "How very few people, especially women, ever reach the state when they do not identify

---

*The word "Essence" is described more fully on Page 55.

with the teacher of the Work". As a psychiatrist he was well aware of "transferences" from patients and of the need to offload them by varying means. In private he asked me, "Do you think I do not know what it is to play the sacrificial fool?" Self-love and vanity did not stand in his way when such a performance was required.

The same pupil recalls a conversation in which Nicoll refers to himself as a "Subtype" of Gurdjieff. He does not elaborate on this remark, but it may relate in some way to a diary note made at an earlier date that reads, "O. was definite. G. was vague; you had to pick it up". I am sure that neither adjective was used in a pejorative sense. There is a difference in emphasis between the two men. Ouspensky's writings show a meticulous accuracy in his thought and his expression of it, whereas Gurdjieff seems to have cared more for what a man was and how he thought rather than for what he thought. Nicoll followed Gurdjieff in this respect when, as he said, he "Painted with words" in order to convey meaning. Often, having "Painted", he would ask "Catch?"; then sometimes sadly, "No catch". It would be a mistake, however, to assume from this that Ouspensky was coldly intellectual. Passages in his book, "Tertium Organum" particularly, show that there was a warmly emotional side to his nature.

Dr. Nicoll did not undervalue the importance of the psychological and cosmological formulations of Gurdjieff's teaching. He presented them faithfully and accurately many times over and woe betide any pupils who distorted them or added frills from his own conceit. When he started writing his "Commentaries" he wrote a note on "Commentary" that for a long time had to be read before reading any other Commentary. This differentiated between the Work ideas and his Commentary on them. He did not wish us to receive the teaching only in our formatory minds but rather to permit it to permeate our being. It was not his role to stuff pupils with information, facts and figures like Gascony geese. The "ideas" provided a scaffolding from which we could observe various features and malfunctioning in our psychology and they also related us to the universe in which we live and the Laws which govern it and us.

The task of a teacher was rather to help his pupils come into their own thinking, feeling and understanding, not to tell them what, or even how, to think and feel. We needed to experience our own lives. Other people's experience might give us a clue sometimes, but we had to awaken to our own innate capacities which are far wider and more meaningful than we think. So the Work teaches awakening from sleep. "Sleep" being the state we ordinarily call being awake, sleep in bed being a physiological necessity.

But a teacher cannot awaken anybody. He can, as Gurdjieff says, only "create conditions" in which a man has a better chance of awakening himself. First he awakens to the fact of sleep, stirs in his sleep and guesses that dreams are dreams.

If Gurdjieff was an artist in creating conditions to remind man of his sleep, both in general and also tailor-made to suit the individual, so was Nicoll in his own way. He sensed the appropriate time and place physically and psychologically to nudge his pupil towards realising his position and his possibility of waking up. However he did not consider himself on the same level as Gurdjieff, whom he acknowledged as "man awake". He wrote in his diary (20.5.52) "In this Work you must not exact or expect from others what you are incapable of yourself; nor must pupils do so of one another. To apply methods to others beyond your level of being is wrong: e.g. to imitate the methods of Gurdjieff means that you are acting beyond your being so it will give wrong results. To demand promises, written or otherwise, is entirely contrary to the original teaching of the Work. No ordinary person can promise anything. G. said, "Can a machine promise? One 'I' may promise when others know nothing about it".

Although Gurdjieff, and Dr. Nicoll on his own level, could only "create conditions", Dr. Nicoll also often spoke of the spermatic influence of the Work. This could promote the growth of spiritual truth in man, or, in other words, his evolution in a vertical dimension or his awakening from sleep, whichever terms you care to employ. The pupil in these special conditions would be more prepared for the reception of these fertilising influences, he would be more likely to have ears to hear and eyes to see and receive the message. In biblical terms he has to hear the knock on the door and then open it of his own free will. There can be no coercion or duress; no threats of hell fire. As in the fairy story Prince Charming may enter to kiss the sleeping princess, when she and the whole court may awaken from their long sleep.

Another use of the metaphor derived from eggs and fertilisation appears in an early diary. "The Institute is a hatching-place for eggs. It supplies the heat. The chicken must try to break the shell. Then help and individual teaching is possible. Until then only collective methods". Conditions may be there; but man is a self-developing organism. This differentiates him from animals. An effort must come from him. He may have a divine hunger deeply buried, but he must dig.

Not much is recorded in Nicoll's personal relationship with Gurdjieff. It is clear that he was considered worthy of "the full treatment" from his teacher and he respected Gurdjieff for supplying it. He came to the conclusion that whilst Gurdjieff acted many roles to produce testing circumstances, these sometimes arose from unpremeditated causes. In either case, the circumstances could be used for work on himself. He described Gurdjieff as "a round man who could not be judged or criticized on any one particular point on his circumference, but only taken as a whole". He considered Gurdjieff a conscious man, but this did not mean that he did not "sleep" at times.

"We think in sensual terms of 'conscious man' as being a large edition of ordinary man, having the same qualities exaggerated, stronger, dominating, cleverer; but he is another kind of man. He might possibly behave oddly and look odd and even seem stupid. In the same way we think sensually that by doing this Work we shall get more and more healthy. But "Physical health closes too often the mind", wrote Dr. Nicoll towards the end of his life. Some of Gurdjieff's manifestations he found repugnant, but his basic sincerity was non-assailable. Some revealing notes from a very early diary, probably written at the Institute, read as follows:—

> "To *be* without associations, e.g. it is late—everything pulls one internally to the idea of tiredness. Late, ought to be in bed, etc. If possible to stop this, not tired. To stop it new life is necessary—quite new ways of life and thought and of what is important—and ultimately this leads to God and the Kingdom of Heaven, i.e. the world does not matter."
>
> "This is energy-releasing thought (1) because if I no longer care in my ordinary ways of caring, (2) because I step outside my circle of limiting ideas, I find myself nearer my living being."

With Ouspensky, there seems to have been a warm "ordinary life" relationship as well as a "Work" relationship. Ouspensky stayed with the Nicolls at their cottage in Siddlesham, was driven around the countryside and entertained in hotels, pubs and restaurants. Sometimes Mme. Ouspensky was with them. Conversations ranged over many subjects, not all serious. However, I think the serious must have predominated for in 1949, after Ouspensky's death, Dr. Nicoll related a dream he had experienced, "Suspensky (sic) is having a good time upstairs. I was at one of his Groups last night. He was paying less attention to rules and having a gay time. He must have taken a leaf out of my book". Nevertheless Dr. Nicoll always acknowledged Ouspensky as one of his teachers and retained a great respect for him.

Dr. Nicoll, in following his own life, had no time for woolly thinking or careless expression of ideas, but was careful to preserve a sense of mystery, to live with a question rather than answer it and to insist on the subordination of words to the meaning they were used to convey.

On the evening before writing these words, I was interested to hear a television debate between three distinguished scientists under an astute chairman. As a non-scientist in almost every respect, I was fascinated by their use of the words "Reductive" and "Constructive" in connection with scientific investigations in exactly the same sense that Dr. Nicoll used them in writing of dream analysis. Furthermore, when pressed as to their willingness to admit possible theological explanations of fundamental problems, they all agreed that there must remain a sense of mystery beyond scientific analysis but doubted the capacity of organised religion to add to their understanding. Whilst I do not pretend to grasp the meaning of such terms as "Deterministic Chaos" the programme as a whole left a pleasant impression that modern scientists were more openminded than I had thought and less glued to the belief that if science does not explain everything today, it will do so tomorrow or soon after. They might accept that with metanoia everything would be seen differently even though not explained.

G. I. Gurdjieff, P. D. Ouspensky, Maurice Nicoll, what giants in understanding.

CHAPTER 4

Early Groups in London

In 1923, Dr. and Mrs. Nicoll left the Institute at Fontainbleau and returned to London, where Dr. Nicoll once again received patients for consultation at 146 Harley Street. They both attended Ouspensky's meetings at Warwick Gardens and received the ideas, formulations, diagrams and cosmology of the Work given in the scrupulously careful manner that belong to Ouspensky. They brought many friends, acquaintances and ex-patients to these meetings. Then in 1931 Nicoll was told, "You had better go away—Go away and teach the system".

From other accounts the parting was abrupt, but it cannot have been quite final because I remember an occasion three or four years later when the Nicoll Group attended a meeting at Warwick Gardens with Ouspensky in the Chair and Dr. Nicoll beside him. There may have been two such meetings. I do not remember much about them except an impression of rather cold formality as compared with our own meetings. Then for many years Mme. Kadloubowski, who, I think, was Ouspensky's secretary, kept an unofficial and kindly contact with the Nicolls. It was her son, George, who as a young architect designed the building that was later erected in Essex and called "Tyeponds". Much later still an old Ouspensky pupil who joined us after Ouspensky's death told me that, when asked about his regrets on parting with Maurice Nicoll, Ouspensky replied, "Well, God gave his only begotten Son". However apocryphal this may be the parting appears to me to have conformed to the "laws" that I suggested earlier would necessitate the severance of a pupil from his teacher as an indispensable condition for his further development.

Dr. Nicoll left all his introductions with Ouspensky and started from "scratch" to build up his own Groups. In the early days a Group contained about twenty to twenty-five people.

At first meetings were held at the house of Mr. Fulford Bush, who, having been a responsive patient, became Dr. Nicoll's first pupil and for a long time his "first lieutenant". Mr. Bush's secretary, was the "dragon at the door" for these early meetings. She was by no means a dragon by nature, but there remained a marked "Ouspensky" flavour in the external organisation at that time. Secrecy was observed. Cars had to be parked a discreet distance from the entrance to the house and pupils did not enter and leave in noticeably large numbers. We would only talk to the outside world about what went on when we did so with the deliberate intention of introducing individuals to the Group. Such new members were also strictly enjoined to attend a fixed number of meetings before they decided to leave and then, if they did so, never to talk about the meetings.

I personally assumed that all this secrecy was "Russian", not knowing any Russians intimately, but having some idea of what they had been through in their own country. Also the dictators of Europe were beginning to emerge. At the same time I understood that the Work required protection from idle chatter and appreciated the condition that the Group had either to talk about the Work, or not to talk about it, but in any case not to interlace our ordinary life conversation with work terminology. When we intended to introduce a friend, we were told to write a brief account of our reasons for thinking that he or she would become suitable material for the Work. Proselytising was generally prohibited. New people were attracted to the Work by "Magnetic Centre", by which they found their way intuitively. "Magnetic Centre" was defined in one way as "The power to differentiate between A and B influences", A influences being those of external mechanical life (render unto Caesar, etc.) and B those emanating from esotericism or the "Conscious Circle of Humanity", first of all as C influences, or conscious influences, but on merging with the material of life becoming diluted to some extent. Examples of B influences are to be found in the words of the great religious teachings, in some old fairy stories and traditional epics. More particularly a new person might be attracted by some of the non-mechanical manifestations of a man in whom the Work had found some root. He would not display his work, so to speak, but sometimes he would not judge quickly, he might listen sometimes instead of talking, but in general he might give an impression of "being at home" in himself from time to time and, while not knowing all the answers, being ready to receive impressions.

Without knowing why, the new person would find his introducer just slightly different and would want to continue the acquaintance.

One of my first introductions was of a young friend who had a county rugger cap. In my early twenties, this made him almost God-like. But he had withdrawn from a county match to attend at some matter concerned with his family business. This indicated that, on quite an ordinary level, he had a scale of priorities. He was not caught up in rugby football. Not being an athlete myself, but having had far distant aspirations of this nature, I doubt whether, in his position, I should not have had my priorities reversed. It was a small thing, but he was interested in serious things and became a useful member of the "Nicoll" Groups.

In the middle thirties, we were more formal than in the post-war years. In meetings we always used the prefixes of Mr., Mrs. or Miss. On longer acquaintance we used Christian names in private. There was no rule about this, but we were reminded that, ideally, Christian names should be "Essence" names and sometimes, as an exercise, to use them carefully, trying to see and hear the more real person behind the name. In practice, of course, Christian names rarely fitted, having been chosen from popular heroes and heroines of the day such as film stars. It was remarkable that sometimes people attracted nicknames that did fit. Surnames were merely an indication of clan or a trade.

I was once reprimanded for using a shortened Christian name in the wrong circumstances. "You damned colonials, always trying to establish a low level of equality and intimacy from the word go." (I am Australian born).

Little by little external rules dropped away. I would like to think that the "Thou shalts" and "thou shalt nots" were dissolved in understanding. Well, perhaps they were to some extent, but on the whole external rules have to be replaced by internal discipline, intelligently and willingly applied to oneself. We tried to apply what was called the science of external impressions. That is we tried to be aware of the impressions we gave to others as well as those that we received of them. Without necessarily changing them, we tried to make objective our postures, intonations, habitual movements, particularly facial ones, our typical phrases and habits of speech. Dr. Nicoll made a note, "Good form—the Englishman's God" and must have regarded it in the same way that

Gurdjieff did "Bon ton", as an absurd master. On the other hand whilst one did not need to become slaves of social convention, the *use* of good manners was a lubricant in a society of sleeping people. Nicoll did not approve of slovenly dress or speech at meetings. We needed to have a sense of occasion and to show respect towards the Work. A sense of balance was necessary and of the desirability of "when in Rome to do as the Romans do". Work people should not stand out from their fellows as peculiar. He had some sympathy for those like pre-war Britons at outposts of Empire who dressed for dinner in the jungle and maintained standards of social convention. Being "asleep" they need external supports. It was better than flopping. He thought that in prisoner of war camps those who kept themselves and their camps clean, shaved, dressed as well as they could, had regular exercises, Church parades and so on, had a far better chance of coming through with a good morale and psychologically undamaged than those who remained scruffy and piled their refuse just outside their huts and let things slide generally. Society needs a structure externally and more so when there is less structure internally.

I was reminded of this on a visit to a Zen monastery in Kyoto where I remarked on the immaculate manner in which the courtyard gravel had been raked and the rocks positioned and asked a monk whether all this was of particular significance. He replied, "Yes. Without external order there can be no internal order. External order will not induce internal order but it will not inhibit it, so that it is more likely to be present".

Nicoll gave me an early example of the necessary relaxation of rules. When I first went to meetings I was living with my parents and was obediently silent about where I went on Thursday evenings and what went on. Not unnaturally my mother was curious and even a little suspicious. When it appeared to worry her, I mentioned it to Dr. Nicoll and said I would like to relieve her distress if I could. He replied, "Talk to her about the Work using the language of Ralph Waldo Trine or Henry Drummond". When I asked how he knew that she read these authors he added that most Victorian ladies of her background often did so. I asked primly, "Is this not insincere and also breaking the rules?". He replied, "No. It may be one of the more sincere of your actions if you do it from understanding. And if you have to read Trine or Drummond to do this you may learn something from it".

My mother and Dr. Nicoll never met, but when in 1947 she was dying Dr. Nicoll used to send her occasional half-bottles of Champagne. Finally amongst her last words to me were "Thank Dr. Nicoll for teaching my children to worry about only the things that are worth worrying about". This was a situation of which only a few were aware. How many others of a similar nature occurred I cannot guess. That was the being of the man.

When I joined the Groups most meetings were being held in a house at Swiss Cottage in North West London. There were two groups at that time and, as numbers increased, a third was added. The teaching was based on the ideas now to be found in Ouspensky's "The Psychology of Man's Possible Evolution" and "In Search of the Miraculous". The teaching was verbal although occasionally a paper was read which much later was recognised as a part of the latter book. We were allowed to take notes and to copy the diagrams from the blackboard, but there was a stern proviso that our notebooks might be confiscated, presumably for destruction. I never heard of this happening.

From our quite early days in a group Dr. Nicoll would have one of the male members sitting beside him behind a small table from where he spoke. Sometimes we were "stooges" who would be required to react to his acting when he wanted to get something over that he could not otherwise portray in plain speech. More often we were asked to start the meeting and collect questions for ten minutes or so before he came in, sometimes replying if we could. At other times we had to continue for a quarter of an hour after he had left the room. We met these tasks with some trepidation, but were supported by the sympathy of the other men who knew that "There but for the grace of God might be I". It was invaluable experience. We learned that meetings were a matter of sharing questions rather than of lecturing each other from a superior standpoint. We learnt to listen and sometimes to search for the meaning behind the words of the question. This helped us to find our own meaning once we had overcome initial nervousness to some extent. It did not come at once, however, for I have read recently some of the reports of those early meetings and have been struck by the adroitness with which we sometimes found appropriate words but missed the real meaning of the question being asked.

There was one occasion in which I was thrown in at the deep

end, so to speak. I had been told to start the meeting and on entering the room I found in front of me a number of familiar faces, familiar from quite another section of my life. Peter Gloster, to whom my everlasting thanks for introducing me to Dr. Nicoll, had rounded up a number of members of the Otter Swimming Club, to which we both belonged. I knew these young men as cheerful, beer-drinking water-polo players and singers of bawdy songs after swimming matches, in many different pubs. Well! It was only going to last ten minutes or so; Dr. Nicoll was in the house. Or so I thought. Having started the meeting and "carried on" for an hour, I closed the meeting saying I thought Dr. Nicoll could not be coming after all. I do not remember seeing any of these "Otters" at meetings again. Mercifully they did not make my Swimming Club life embarrassing thereafter.

At another meeting I was instructed to ask three really stupid questions from the body of the meeting. "I want to use these for the benefit of somebody else", Dr. Nicoll said. "I shall probably blow you up, but you will understand". As the meeting moved towards its close, I caught Dr. Nicoll's eye and had not asked the first stupid question. Finally I knew whose vanity would not allow him to appear stupid and for whose benefit the instruction had been given.

When words were inadequate Dr. Nicoll, as I have said, would act. I remember him picking up the table in front of him and trying to walk through the door, complaining bitterly that "They always build these damned doors too narrow". The stooge would say, "But why not put the table down?" The reply to this was, "What table? This is I, Dr. Nicoll". He was referring to the doctrine of Essence and Personality, Essence being the simple, but real thing with which we are born as babies and Personality as the fat coating of material acquired from subsequent life, our education, acquired morals, social attitudes, professional qualifications, fixed opinions and many other things which, properly, should form food for Essence to grow from, but have usurped the active role from that which is *real* so that Essence becomes passive to this acquired material. The "Persona" or mask plays the actor. Although parts of Personality are not harmful in themselves, the reversal of relationship can lead to the eventual suffocation of Essence—which is death—or a walking automaton.

The idea of "Rich Man" in the Gospels is precisely the same.

It is easier for a camel to go through the eye of a needle than for him to enter the Kingdom of Heaven. Likewise Alice in Wonderland had to drink of the reducing medicine before she could pass through the small entrance to the garden.

How often we were told to wake up in the morning, put on the appropriate material clothing for the day and put on the appropriate psychological clothing for the situation, but we wearing it instead of it wearing us. Unless we can become "as little children" psychologically and could "wash each other's feet" we have no chance of waking up to what is real in ourselves and of growing from that.

The Groups were small and our teacher's time and force was directed towards individuals as well as to the Group as a whole. It was an extraordinarily rich period for many of us. None of us were allowed to feel special but were candidates for learning how to awaken ourselves from "sleep".

Sometimes after meetings Dr. Nicoll would take quite a number of us to the old Cafe Royal for supper where we would sit on the plush seats at marble-top tables. The conversation was bright and ranged widely. Looking round the neighbouring tables, he would tell us of the relationship between other diners, their difficulties and psychological states merely from what he saw as he looked at them, from their boredom, vivacity and other tell-tale hints. Whether strictly accurate or not, it was an education for the surrounding and admiring "Dr. Watsons".

Teaching was in everything—not just in words. I was told later, when given some responsibility of my own, "When taking a meeting and using "Work" words such as "identifying", "negative emotion", "self-justifying", "internal considering", "inner talking", "making accounts", and so on, you must have the taste of the experience belonging to these expressions in your being as you speak. If the words become jargon and rattle down like peas on a plate, you will convey nothing. And if this rule keeps you silent, it might be no bad thing". One finds that it is tempting to imagine that one is speaking with the tongues of men and of angels sometimes and then it is salutary to remember that without "Agape" it will be like tinkling cymbals and sounding brass as St. Paul wrote to the Corinthians. "Love" here means something far bigger than oneself and should lie behind the meaning that the words convey.

As in the middle nineteen-thirties the consulting rooms in Harley Street were still in use, we were encouraged to ring up and make appointments as though we were patients—but without the fees. The conversations there could last for minutes or hours according to the freedom and quality of the flow of thoughts. I did not take advantage of this opportunity very frequently, but when I did these visits were of inestimable value. We were allowed to think and express our own thoughts and a lot of useless junk was swept away. It was an unusual experience to find someone actually listening to what I said and then to find the ability to listen myself to what was said to me.

On one such visit Dr. Nicoll opened the conversation by saying, "If we really inhabited our time-bodies we should now be able to pick up the threads of our last conversation from the exact point where we left off".

It may have been on the same occasion that, sitting beside his desk, I found my finger tracing the moulding around the edge of the desk as we talked. Considering this to be a useless mechanical manifestation not becoming to an aspirant for more conscious behaviour, I stopped it abruptly. Dr. Nicoll laughed, "No. Don't stop. Give the dog a bone. It is more important to keep the train of thought alive than to stop this action which keeps Moving Centre happy and does not use much force".

He smoked very small pipes, or more accurately, he kept on filling them as he talked, spilling tobacco down his waistcoat and lighting matches which often went out before he applied them to the pipe. His talk was always interesting in these circumstances and I wondered whether he was giving bones to dogs, or giving us reason to doubt his degree of consciousness, or just being mechanical.

Of smoking, he said that many more people were addicted to the Moving Centre habit of filling and lighting pipes, taking our cigarettes and tapping them on the case and so on, than were addicted to nicotine. These little operas filled in awkward moments and covered embarrassment in social surroundings or reproduced the actions of a favourite film-star, whilst pipes added to the masculine image. I had started to smoke at this time—a pipe—and asked whether it was a good or bad thing to do. "I don't know. It may help you to relax sometimes but if you hold strong views against smoking you will have to smoke".

This period in my life was important for the help I received in making objective and improving my relationship with my father. We had some differences over my matrimonial intentions and I was tempted to speak plainly, walk out and tell him what to do with the traditional shilling. But Dr. Nicoll advised "Your father is old and dying. It is far more important that he should die at peace with you than that you should blurt out what you consider to be the blunt truth and have your way immediately. There is a better truth than that. Play along with him. Bring him round to your point of view and your fiancée must help in this. She must captivate him. This will be Work and I shall work with you. If you 'will' and feel the necessity for this course of action it will be a more true sincerity". I had not allowed that my father was also acting mechanically from what was laid down in him by a puritanical north-country upbringing and would be as glad as I to be let off the hook of this over-dramatised situation. It turned out well; but how easily it might have been otherwise.

There is an aphorism that "Your being attracts your life", i.e. what you *are* attracts what happens to you. While "Essence" is under the law of "Fate" (or design) Personality is under many other laws, including "Law of Accident". At the time of which I am writing so many things of significance came together and my contact with Dr. and Mrs. Nicoll was particularly influential so that it seemed that there was a guiding spirit somewhere and that for the time being the accidental was less in evidence than the "fatal" or essential. I saw much that was subsequently clouded over by the requirements of Personality and self-love. There was mystery in life.

We were also told that it is a mistake to protect a man from the consequences of his being. If, by Work, he can change his being, he can learn from what happens. But the change cannot be made for him. Yet Dr. Nicoll appeared to be doing just this in the circumstances I have mentioned and no doubt in others connected with other pupils. Could it be said, I wondered, that in some cases our being attracted Dr. Nicoll's intervention? Did *his* being require the employment of his influence in the design? He himself would disclaim the power to *do*, but sometimes the power "to let be done" that which in time and place is law-conformable.

Another example of Nicoll's penetration into my life related to the habits of thrift which had been instilled by my father, whose favourite mottoes were "Study what you can do without and not with" and "Look after the pence and the pounds will look after themselves". I was told to work against my acquired mechanicalness of thrift and self-deprivation and substitute the feeling that I had a right to have what I wanted—and have it. This might continue for a long time. For another person his private line of work might lie in a diametrically opposite direction, that is to relinquish the feeling that he has a divine right to have what he wants just as soon as he wants it. This exemplified the principle that general rules and general tasks are unsuitable since everyone's work is different on the manifest level. I quote from another pupil's reminiscences, "For Y, yes, it would be good to keep silent. For X, she should talk more, really learn to express herself in conversation and communicate more with others".

One of Dr. Nicoll's favourite aphorisms was "Serious things cannot be understood without laughable things". The same pupil recalls the following, "Down here we laugh a lot, play a lot, but only because it is so very serious. To enjoy oneself is the result of conscious effort. Take nothing seriously except the Work". A pupil might say "Dr. Nicoll, I want to have a serious talk with you. I have a serious problem". "Have a glass of wine", Dr. Nicoll would answer in the tradition of Ouspensky, realising that nothing could be achieved whilst the other was in a state of identification. He would annoy them by ignoring the "serious problem" and talking about something apparently superficial. Only later would the pupil realise that owing to the force of Dr. Nicoll's being, his relationship to the problem had completely changed.

To illustrate some of the things that amused Dr. Nicoll, here are some extracts from his diaries and reported conversations that caught his sense of fun:

> "She was in possession of all his faculties."
>
> "He was all things to all women."
>
> "The woman who wanted to be liked but did not know how to be likeable."
>
> "All bright eyed and bushy tailed" (Kevin O'Hara).
>
> Mrs. Marx of her husband, "He wrote a book about capital, but we have not a penny."
>
> "I am an upright man, a downright man, a forthright man, an always bloody well right man."

"Freud Fish."

"You must believe in God, my dear, in spite of what the clergy say of him" (Jowett).

These are gleaned from different sources. The "upright man" was clearly his own.

CHAPTER 5

Lakes Farm and Tyeponds

At the same time that meetings were being held in London, work of a more physical nature was being conducted in Essex. Mrs. Pogson has described Tyeponds in her book, but since she was not among the earliest on the scene, I am including here an account by Miss Hester Lord who joined the Group in the early thirties and took an active part in the building of the house and the ancillary activities from the very beginning. It is written from an essentially feminine point of view and gives a picture of Dr. and Mrs. Nicoll so alive and warm that no one could imagine it proceeding from a masculine pen. It is given with her permission in full and without editing. There are now very few people who remember those days from direct experience, having taken such a continuous and active part in all that went on.

Recollections of Dr. and Mrs. Nicoll

I asked permission to go to Lakes Farm, Dr. Nicoll's weekend home near Rayne, Braintree, a few weeks after the building of the "Work" house had started.

Dr. Nicoll had received a gift of money from a member of the Work, Miss Wadham, with which to buy the field behind the farm. In this field the house was to be built. In a small pond in the field there grew a weed called "Tyeponds" and the house was named after it.

A few people were allowed to go each week to help build. Accommodation was limited so, at first, only three or four people went down to stay at the farm. Later Mr. Bush had a wooden hut, "Apple Tree Cottage". Later still Miss Corcoran had another hut, "Walnut Tree Cottage". At some time during the early days of building the Parfits bought a cottage nearby, which later was to belong to Miss Kent and Miss Powell had a house built. Sunday Wilshin and "Moxy" came over regularly from their cottage at Little Bardfield. Some of us who were younger slept, that first summer, in the summer house or in a tent. We were taken to the farm by those members of the Group who had cars. Later Winifred Park, with whom I then lived and who had brought me into the Work, found the invaluable "Hicks Brothers Bus" which left for Rayne on Friday evenings at six o'clock from Gower Street, taking two hours. So we frequently travelled down by bus on Friday evenings arriving at the farm before anyone else.

Dr. and Mrs. Nicoll usually came down quite early on Saturday morning in time to go shopping for the weekend. Sometimes Dr. Nicoll came down on Friday by himself when he had had a very busy week and then he would sleep until quite late on Saturday morning to catch up with lost sleep. He once told me that he could put off sleep for several nights if necessary but had to make it up later. Sometimes in beautiful weather, to our surprise and joy, they both came down quite early on Friday and were there when we arrived.

I was allowed to go down the week after I had asked if I might (I think because I had said I could sleep in my brother's small tent!). When I arrived, very frightened, I was most warmly greeted by Mrs. Nicoll, whom I had previously thought, at meetings, to be very aloof. Later, I realised that she was shy. I had been told to bring my "weaving things" and I well remember Dr. Nicoll's real, or simulated interest in my home-made distaff and spindle and "waist loom" and his attempts to spin.

In the morning I was required to help cook the breakfast; the prospect of frying six eggs, or more was daunting; Mrs. Casswell, in charge and very kind, did her best to put me at ease, but I clearly remember the effect that Dr. Nicoll had on me—and continued to have for some years—so that I would not answer his questions by "yes" or "no" but always had to explain. This was, still is when I am identified, a characteristic that I saw at that breakfast clearly for the first time. I speak of this because I think that this was the sort of immediate impact that Dr. Nicoll had on most people, through his own great awareness.

We were to start to make a shed which was to house the tools for building. This shed (later to become a bedroom and finally the Weaving Shed) was right up the field, close to where the house would be built. The foundations had already been dug, Dr. and Mrs. Nicoll both taking part, as they were young and vigorous. He was not slim but was sturdily built (he described himself as being "a tall short man) and to see him digging, the inevitable pipe in his mouth, with the other men and women was always a "homely" sight, nothing Olympian—and yet he was Olympian.

This morning we were to lay a course of bricks upon which to construct the shed. As always a little ceremony was held; this gaiety was an integral part of both their natures—a lightness of touch which was so often manifested. Amidst a small but admiring crowd Mrs. Nicoll laid the first brick. Then Mrs. Parfit laid two more. Interest waning I was left to continue the row while others went off to other jobs. I was, as always, afraid of not doing it well enough and what with careful placing and replacing of each brick and constant use of the spirit level, when Dr. Nicoll returned after about half an hour, I had laid five bricks! Now I realise how amused and perhaps exasperated he must have been, for in some respects he was a very impatient man, but he explained very gently that if I were as meticulous as that we should be a very long time building the shed, let alone the house. He then laid several to show me the way and then left me to it. The brick laying continued much more speedily.

I remember a very good lunch, cooked, I expect, by Mrs. Nicoll and Mrs. Parfit. (Mrs. Nicoll, who was an excellent cook, told me later that when they returned to England after being at the Institute she just could not cook at all and they had to have all meals sent in for a time.) Before the meal all the women, and men too I suppose, were expected to wash and tidy themselves and (the women) as Mrs. Nicoll put it "to make beauty". This was always the case—at Tyeponds, The Knapp, Quaremead and Great Amwell; and a very gracious custom it was. Always there was a mirror in the kitchen! Dr. Nicoll was emphatic that "grace" was important to everyday living. He once said that it was like "grease"—it eased the wheels to turn smoothly. He also said that women had a difficult role to play in life; they must develop their intellectual centre (and he could become very impatient with those who made no effort to do so), use their brains, but never forget to be "gracious", "graceful" in life. Women, he said, in any community set the standard for men. Mrs. Nicoll later connected this with Gurdjieff's saying that one result of the Work should be that women became more womanly and men more manly. In this connection Dr. Nicoll always came to take meetings looking very well groomed and expected all men who took meetings to do likewise—and all who came to them—as a mark of respect to the Work.

I think he positively enjoyed cleanliness and one of my cherished recollections is to see him—as I clearly can—in white shirt and flannels, panama hat on head, pipe in mouth, hands in pockets, snow white "pumps" on feet walking across the field (or across the kitchen floor I had just washed), followed by Pushti his dog. Pushti-Koo-Mitra, he said was Persian for "Prince from over the Hills" and Pushti, of doubtful origin, certainly had Borzoi blood and carried himself with his plumed tail as proudly as any prince. He had been bought as a puppy for Jane (his daughter) but had long since become Dr. Nicoll's dog, following him around wherever possible and guarding his ancient car when parked in Harley Street. Dr. Nicoll had beautiful, workmanlike, strong hands, the left seldom being clean on the inside because he so often knocked his pipe out into the palm. He nearly always looked immaculate, digging, laying bricks, sawing or directing the placing of the various beams and rafters. He always wore very thinly soled shoes or rubbers as he liked to receive impressions from the ground. It was interesting to see him walking across a ploughed field shod in white "pumps", where most people would undoubtedly prefer thick shoes.

I cannot remember clearly anything more about that first weekend (from which I have digressed considerably) except that I came back knowing that this was my "home" and that never in my life, except in my own home, had I ever experienced such a feeling of warmth and love as that which was generated by Dr. and Mrs. Nicoll. Other days, other weekends and longer holidays have merged together in my mind, so I will content myself with setting out various incidents.

The tool shed was soon finished and the house started. It gradually grew long and low and gracious along the side of the field. There were five courses of bricks upon which we cemented sills and then a wooden framework to take the lath and plaster walls. Men and women fetched and carried, mixed cement and later plaster, sawed and hammered alike, and worked together in, as far as I can remember, harmony and fellowship. (I think I was too concerned with "Miss Lord" and too generally afraid to notice others and their reactions very much). I loved Dr. Nicoll dearly from the very beginning and always shall, but it certainly could not have been perfect love because it did not "cast out all fear". I think many people had similar feelings, for he could be unpredictable and fiercely spoken, although I hope more courageous than I. I had no fear of Mrs. Nicoll—just a great love.

I remember wondering why, whenever I met Dr. Nicoll walking from the farm to the house, he always looked so worried. It was years before I realised that he was being a "mirror" to me! I remember a time when we were both standing in the field talking in friendly fashion when someone arrived whom he wished to shock. I knew that he was completely sober, but, when he went to greet this man he acted and talked to him as if he were half drunk. I was amazed and about as shocked as the man. It was marvellous acting. I often wondered afterwards when he appeared to be the worse for drink how much was acting—although I am aware it often was not. He once said that he had to drink in order to be able to tell people what he had to tell them, or to give them a jolt out of their self complacency. Much later, at Great Amwell House, Mrs. Nicoll said to me early one evening, "Maurice says we are going to have a bad time tonight dear; Mr. — has brought a girl he is thinking of marrying and she won't do at all. He is going to put her off". He did. We had a "drunk" and lewd evening—one of the worst I can remember; nothing more was heard of the girl although the young man remained with us for several years.

After the wooden framework of the house had been erected there was a great storm and high winds blew across the flat Essex plain; when we arrived the next weekend the whole skeleton of the house sloped over towards the west. We stood looking at it in dismay. Not so Dr. Nicoll; he had some very strong rope brought. One end was fastened to the top corner of the house opposite the slope and the other end to a strong peg hammered deep into the ground. The rope had been doubled. The men put a strong iron bar between the two pieces of rope and twisted it and so twisted the rope. It took several men straining on the bar—Dr. Nicoll calling out directions and encouragement. Gradually, amidst cheers, the whole house came back into true against the plumb line. Then everyone present set about fixing diagonal struts and cross struts and so on—tea was brought into the field and we all worked without ceasing until all danger of collapse was over. We were up soon after six the next morning and during that Sunday and for several succeeding weekends hundreds of laths were nailed to the struts. Then we began to plaster the outside of the house. Then it was realised that so much plaster was falling through (at great expense) that after that we put ruberoid between the laths and the struts.

We all mixed plaster, regardless of age or sex, and what painful holes it made in the finger tips until one learned to wear rubber gloves! I remember once while wielding a very heavy spade saying to myself—aloud—"Bring some more cement". Dr. Nicoll, who was passing by at that moment, looked extremely surprised but obediently brought it. I tried, as usual, to explain but was cut short with exasperated amusement.

Then we began to do some work inside, putting in floor boards on the ground floor, then making the room divisions and putting up the ceilings. At one point the County Surveyor came to "pass" the house. He was well plied with sherry by Dr. Nicoll before coming up to the house, otherwise he might have shown more reluctance to pass it – the foundations were rather meagre in some parts. There was a second storey but this was passed for store rooms only. This was agreed to, but when the Inspector had gone, Dr. Nicoll decided to "store" sleeping bodies up there and the Surveyor never returned to inspect. I was required to paint red and orange flames on a fire door between two of these store rooms.

We made the doors, cut the glass for the window panes and hung the windows. Plasterboard was put in for the downstairs ceilings and I remember Dr. Nicoll's look of horror, followed by gales of laughter, as a foot and leg came through the ceiling of Room 2 as someone upstairs trod on the plasterboard instead of a beam. I remember the beautifully shaped "Lion Room" over the big room (first the exercise room, later the dining room). Dr. Nicoll had in an old book a picture of a lion whose paws had been cut off and placed in the four corners of the picture. I had to enlarge this and then Miss Wadham carved it in plaster in semi-relief. It was placed on the main wall of the room—"Strength without Violence".

I think it was eighteen months later that we had our first Christmas in the new house. There were about thirty-six of us—a lot for those days—we all wore evening dress, at least the women did. There were beautiful table decorations with huge red lighted candles, but one stepped out of the dining room straight into the snowy field! It was this Christmas or perhaps a later one that Dr.

Nicoll gave every woman a present, a thermometer, saying no woman knew how to keep a room at a decent temperature but roasted everyone.

How cold it could be on that Essex plain! I did not think anyone could possibly have been as cold as I was, puttying windows outside in an east wind. But Dr. Nicoll saw that we always had hot coffee before returning home. In those days we had no central heating, that came much later. However we had a Triplex grate in the kitchen which was finished long before the rest of the house. We cooked on the Triplex and in the side oven and we also had two "Florence" oil stoves with ovens on top. On these we cooked many magnificent meals. I remember very well how one very cold day Marjorie Hodder, who was assistant cook, thickened the white sauce with soap powder. We came in, half frozen, to what we thought was a delicious meal—I think it was roast lamb with haricot beans in a white sauce. As we were served and started to eat silence fell upon the table and knives and forks were put down. Dr. Nicoll, who was talking and had not started his lunch, felt the silence, looked around, tried his meal and ejaculated something I could not hear but I am sure was unprintable and demanded to know who had used soap. Plates were cleared away—I think some of us were privately thankful that it would not be "Work" to eat the meal. We had bread and cheese followed by one of the most stimulating Work talks that I can remember. (In those days we did not have meetings at Tyeponds but in London during the week). When he had finished, Dr. Nicoll smiled around at the company and said, "That is instead of your lunch". I think I should say in passing that since then Mrs. Hodder has always tasted meals before serving them and is an excellent cook.

Sometime during this period David Squire, one of the younger men, dug a twelve foot deep well—water having been found by a water diviner—this was later deepened mechanically and we had a real bathroom. A bath however was always something of an event—not to say ceremony. Usually we carried water to the wash basins in the bedrooms. The Elsans were further up the field. Two young men, brought by Peter Gloster, were given the task of making a sort of sentry box for a new Elsan. To everyone's amusement when we came down the next weekend we found that the weather boarding overlapped the wrong way up thus ensuring that rain would drip down inside! Dr. Nicoll, who was highly amused by this, insisted that Mr. Gloster should take the weather boarding off and replace it correctly. This he did with good grace explaining to all and sundry that he was on work of National Importance.

For lighting we used oil lamps in the kitchen and dining room and mostly candles in the bedrooms. Very often Miss Park and I would go down by bus on Friday night, wash the lamp glasses and fill the lamps; then, in the morning, we would sweep the big room and wash the kitchen floor. About eleven o'clock Dr. and Mrs. Nicoll and Pushti would arrive bringing us much joy. Often one of us would go shopping—usually Miss Park—with them or one of them in the car to Braintree.

I remember, one weekend I stayed at Tyeponds working, feeling rather annoyed with myself because I had forgotten to bring any toothpaste and also forgotten to ask Miss Park to buy some. When they returned Dr. Nicoll said, "Lord I have brought you some toothpaste". When I told him why I was so pleased with my present he was delighted with this example of synchronicity. These always pleased him and I know of more events similar to this.

When the "big" room was finished we had various types of exercise—Judo, Health and Beauty and, later, Work Exercises on Saturday evenings. Often after the exercises were over we would talk, or rather Dr. Nicoll would talk and we would listen standing up around him, far into the night. Then after a few hours' rest we would get up for Sunday's work.

Sometimes if something urgent were needed we would have a "scurry". In that case we got up at six o'clock and worked all out until lunch and again after lunch probably until five. But although we were worked very hard, Dr. Nicoll was far from unobservant of our physical state. I remember one Saturday morning when he arrived I was sent firmly off to bed and told not to get up until time to go home on Sunday. This was a much needed rest for me but we were all enveloped in his and Mrs. Nicoll's loving care and felt the warmth of their beings.

In the early days before the war, when he was younger, I was afraid of him—to a lesser extent I always was—and I think many people were although he was not as violent as he sometimes was at the Knapp. But this fear was, to a large extent, because of his stature. But always I felt, in spite of this and I think also many others did, a certain odd sense of ease because he knew so much about me—the weaknesses, the jealousies, the fears, the vanities—but there was no need for pretence. I knew he knew me better than I knew myself, accepted me and loved me in spite of all this.

At times one was almost completely at ease and filled with happiness. I remember one such occasion when Mrs. Nicoll was away and he was staying down at the farm, Mrs. Elliott and I cooked a duck for him and for Michael Streatfield as a lovely surprise. They arrived, anticipating a good lunch, at one o'clock, but unfortunately it was not cooked—and it wasn't cooked until half past two. But, thanks entirely to him, neither of us were identified and we passed the time gaily drinking wine and listening to him telling stories; somehow it was a very special duck. Another time, early in the evening, when I thought I was alone at Tyeponds, he suddenly appeared having come down alone from London. I slipped out to the village, bought chops and tomatoes and invited him to supper. He was very pleased, brought up a bottle of wine from the farm and we cooked the meal together. When we had eaten it we washed up together and then walked over the ploughed fields (both plimsoled) to visit Madame K. and her husband. One never forgets such events—and many of us cherish some or other of this kind and will always. It was both a pleasure and an education to go shopping with him; everyone who served him was given real attention and interest and left feeling the happier for his visit. It was the same in the pub; when he talked to the local people he took a genuine interest in them, their pursuits, their problems and quietly helped any who needed help. When someone in the Group was scornful about a plaster roundel one of them had made and painted, he rounded on him asking him what he could do and if he could do it as well.

As the Group grew larger and more people wanted to come down for the weekend, a much larger extension was built by a local builder at right angles to the house. It was convenient, if not well designed, with a fair number of bedrooms, a balcony and a large downstairs room for exercises. It made life easier but never had the same feeling as the original house.

Work exercises then became an important and for most of us much looked forward-to end to Saturday nights. At first Dr. Nicoll took them, afterwards Mrs. Curry. We seemed to continue sometimes for hours. The Dervish Prayer often went on for twenty minutes or more, and so generated enormous force. Then we would drink tea in the kitchen and laugh easily so that the force did not turn sour.

Earlier than this we spent many busy evenings making cross stitch rugs, Dr. and Mrs. Nicoll and all the men sewing with us. But as soon as there was room we started weaving. The tool shed had become a bedroom but when the extension was built it became the weaving shed. Here we had three foot looms, one of them being a beautiful Swedish loom capable of weaving cloth 54 inches wide; if necessary two people could sit on the bench working together. Here Winifred Park and I, who both knew a fair amount about weaving, wove warm woollen curtains for Dr. Nicoll's room at Lakes Farm—orange curtains which he tied back with pink ribbon until I wove him some ties. We wove rugs for the bedrooms, I wove a stair carpet for the front stairs and Mary Reekie a far more beautiful one, inspired by alpine flowers, for the back. Then we wove pale golden curtains with bands of "Solomon's Seal" for the exercise room.

Dr. Nicoll was very interested and pleased about this. He often came into the weaving shed to stand and watch us and watch our rather feeble attempts at spinning. He painted a sort of Grecian picture of Miss Park on the door of the shed. Various women learnt to weave, but no men. Later several of us tried our hands at carving and carved a "vine" board to go across the front of the house. We also carved the stair posts. Mrs. Nicoll was very good at this. (I think it was later, at Quaremead, that we carved a Nativity scene).

He said everyone should be in touch with the earth and able to do weaving and spinning and gardening and other crafts. Mrs. Nicoll loved gardening and was a very good gardener but he was never seen working in the garden! I often wondered why he never seemed to think dressmaking was a useful craft—and so did Mrs. Nicoll. He encouraged us to paint; he painted very well himself and sometimes we had lessons from members of the Group who were artists. We also had guitar lessons and he, who played well (as a child he had learnt to play the violin) used to sing and accompany himself or accompany Sunday Wilshin singing Spanish songs—Hasta la Manana, Juanita, She is a Flower, and so on. He was impatient with those of us who wouldn't, or couldn't sing. He seemed not to believe that one just couldn't pitch the right note!

All this stopped for a time when war was declared. Dr. and Mrs. Nicoll, Mrs. Maffett and Mrs. Riley and their children, Mrs. Pogson (who became Dr. Nicoll's secretary) and a few other people went to live at Tyeponds and Lakes Farm. Here they received "evacuees"—expectant mothers and some children, most of whom didn't like the country and found their "billets" primitive.

I don't know much about this time. I think I managed to get there only twice. One occasion was when I was in considerable professional difficulties, owing to the effect of war strain upon a lightly balanced headmistress. Dr. Nicoll was extraordinarily kind, understanding and helpful—although I suspect he went away at one point to conceal his amusement!

When France fell Dr. and Mrs. Nicoll and various members of the Group went to the Knapp, in Birdlip, Gloucestershire. Shortly afterwards the King's Head Cottage, then empty, was rented and several of us sent our furniture there. The two houses became a refuge for various people and the rest of us went there when we could manage to do so.

* * * * * * *

For my own part contact with Lakes Farm started with (I think) that first Christmas that Hester Lord mentions. My sister and I motored down to Rayne on Christmas day, arriving in time for the evening festivities. This was early in our "Work" careers and I, for one, wondered how people trying to be conscious would approach the festivities; perhaps there would be no time for frivolity. What I did not expect was the extraordinary warmth of welcome and hospitality that greeted us. There were masses of traditional food and wine with presents for all. The men were given copies of Mandeville's "Fable of the Bees".

Some of us were boarded at the local pub, for Lakes Farm was a small building and Tyeponds not yet built. The Nicolls were generous and at first Dr. Nicoll seemed to find difficulty in demanding cash. They simply liked giving. When the building of Tyeponds commenced the demand was unavoidable. Even after that there was a reading from an Ouspensky paper every six months or so on what Gurdjieff called "The Material Question". This described the psychological need for the demand for money as well as the material. People were asked to subscribe to the Group generally and not for specific objects and to give according to their evaluation of what they received from the Work. As a rule people do not value what they do not pay for and payment was necessary whether a material need existed or not.

It was a principle that whatever work we did either at Tyeponds or in London should not be seen as an end in itself but only as a means. The whole of our work, in fact, was only a means, but it gave us a sense of direction. Direction towards what? That could never be encapsulated in words. Can an egg or a caterpillar say what it means to be a butterfly? One could have signposts on the way and move from one to the next. We could say we aim to be awake, for higher consciousness or use some other phrase, but in sleep or unconsciousness we could not know what these states might be, only that they must be something different from what we experience as we are now.

Then we were told that the real field for practical work is in the life we are given day by day. Group work provided special conditions in which we might glimpse the possibility of another way of being and of understanding, but if we were to live only in these conditions we might resemble long, weak hothouse plants with little chance of survival when planted out in the harsh conditions of the outside world. The Work is the way in the midst of life.

We were also told not to work for results. Something looking like results might appear on the way: these would be relative and temporary and not to be rested upon. Everything remained in flux. Mrs. Nicoll sent us a picture postcard of a gipsy caravan with the message, "Perhaps us next time".

"Sergeant majors" were appointed for the day or for a particular job. They were not always selected for technical skills. Sometimes, it would seem, for the opposite reasons. Perfectionists had to endure the inefficiency of the ham-fisted whilst the vague and inefficient suffered from the fastidious requirements of the perfectionists. Your colleague might be the last person you would have selected to work alongside. Friction was an indispensable ingredient of Work at times. Observing the other person in yourself and you in him was a much work as hammering nails into wood. The other person reflects a projection of your unacknowledged dark side, thus providing knowledge indispensable for ultimate freedom.

When scurries were the order of the day we were expected to work at double the usual pace. It was surprising how this sometimes improved the quality of our work. We had less time for dreaming and occasionally found a rhythm which would otherwise be lacking.

"Come on! Get it up. You are not building for posterity".

During one such scurry I had made a frame for a dormer window and was about to attach it to the roof when I was told to give it to someone else to finish. Then Dr. Nicoll said "It is a lovely day. Would you not like to take your fiancée for a walk across the fields? Take her over that way". "That way" was in full view of all the men working on the roof and it goes without saying I was not to explain my gross neglect of duty to the others. Nor was I afterwards able to look at the dormer window and say "all my own work". My self-love, my darling image had to suffer.

It is not quite true to say that Dr. Nicoll left Tyeponds without a backward glance because he did return when the war was over to see what possessions remained of those that had been left behind. Nevertheless he was singularly unattached to material possessions. Moreover he was persuaded that a part of the art of living was expressed in the third chapter of Ecclesiastes, "To everything there is a season and a time for every purpose under Heaven. A time to be born, a time to die, a time to plant, a time to pluck up that which is planted . . ." Regret or resentment were a useless waste of energy. The present moment was the only place "to be". From "now" you may look back, with attention, in to the past, or forward into the future, say to plan. But you work from here and now. The same chapter of Ecclesiastes has the words, "That which has been is now and that which is to be hath already been". This is time seen as a dimension and my life in time as a dimension of my being. To those in love, in the conventional meaning of the phrase, Dr. Nicoll would warn, "There will be times when you can say almost anything and you will not be misunderstood. Other times when your lightest word will be misunderstood. Be sensitive to the possibilities of the moment. Logical argument will avail nothing".

Of the houses where Work was carried on, at Tyeponds,

Birdlip, Quaremead and Amwell he would reiterate "The Work is not a building, a place, a book, a system, dogma or tradition. The Work is something that lives in the hearts of men—if they can find it".

There is an interesting note recorded on 20.11.44, "School is outside time and space in the realm of psychological experience, new insight and understanding; not of bricks and mortar on earth. The object of a School on earth is to open the mind to feel those influences that come down from conscious humanity at the level of the Sun".

CHAPTER 6

Birdlip and the Commentaries

When Tyeponds was taken over by the army at short notice, the Nicolls and some of the women surrounding them moved to the village of Birdlip in Gloucestershire. The Nicolls and those without children occupied a rented house half way down Birdlip Hill, whilst mothers with children were housed in a former public house, the Kings Head, at the top of the hill.

Although my wife and children were there for a period, I only managed to visit Birdlip on two occasions, being caught up in war service. So I cannot write much from personal experience.

I know that Dr. Nicoll felt it necessary to be "Father" to the children. In the family, as in Society generally, there needed to be some sort of structure and "Father" stood for authority. He was the final arbiter in important matters and from time to time dealt out punishment and reward. The mothers bore the daily burden of their children but sometimes needed support from an authority beyond their own, in their husbands' absence.

It happened that five of the women in the party were named Dorothy and Dr. Nicoll was known to sigh, "All these Gifts of God . . ." alluding to the Greek derivation of the name.

More seriously he made it his daily task to "visualise" all the absent husbands and other members of the Group and to hold them in his consciousness for a short while.

At this time he started writing papers which later came to be called "Psychological Commentaries on the Teaching of Gurdjieff and Ouspensky". These "Commentaries" have recently been published in paperback edition and on this occasion I was asked to write a short review for the quarterly magazine "Light". I reproduce it here.

"It is good news that Dr. Maurice Nicoll's 'Commentaries' have been republished in paperback and will be more readily available than in recent years. These volumes were born of necessity: originally a series of papers written in the early days of the war when members of the Nicoll Groups were widely dispersed in the forces and elsewhere and travelling was difficult. Dr. Nicoll had moved from London to Birdlip and provided a refuge for some of the wives and children attached to the Group as well as a meeting place for those on leave who could find petrol coupons and otherwide to overcome the difficulties of travel. The papers were widely distributed so that, where possible, distant members could meet to discuss them and keep a common line of work alive amongst themselves. The contents were based upon the meetings held at Birdlip and the Work conducted by Dr. Nicoll amongst the people immediately around him. This probably accounts for the liveliness and immediacy that makes the "Commentaries" unique amongst books written by others than Gurdjieff and Ouspensky themselves, about their teaching. It should be remembered Ouspensky's "In Search of the Miraculous" and Gurdjieff's "All and Everything" were not published in England until 1949 and 1950 respectively, whereas all the wartime Commentaries had been privately published in 1949.

"Maurice Nicoll wrote from the experience of the day with a kind of alchemy that could transmute the base metal of humdrum life into the gold of a different quality of experience without necessarily changing external circumstances; a change of inner attitude. It seems that Nicoll had assimilated the essence of Gurdjieff's method into his being. The papers continued after the war when groups reassembled at Amwell House and some pupils had been delegated to conduct sub-groups in other places. Once again they provided a common line of work.

"Knowing the conditions in which these papers were written, readers may be willing to accept repetition where it occurs. Dr. Nicoll wrote from a definite place in space and time and a definite place in his psychology on each occasion.

"For some time we were obliged to read the short "Introduction to the Commentaries" (Vol.1, p.15) before proceeding to another Commentary. The writer was anxious that his commentary should not be confused with 'The Work' itself. The formulations, diagrams and cosmology were to remain inviolate and not subject to ornamentation or change at the whim of a sub-group leader. Nevertheless the Commentary insists that one object of the Work is to make people think for themselves from the ideas.

"Truth is truth and there is no copyright when a man sees it for himself and it becomes a part of his being. He will remain ever grateful to the guide who led him to the truth. But henceforth it is his own. In such a way Dr. Nicoll assimilated the truth and goodness of the 'Work', as the Gurdjieff teaching is usually called, and he became a transmitter for the benefit of others who had ears to hear what he was saying. Very many people remain inexpressibly thankful for his existence. Perhaps the paperback Commentaries will expand their number, particularly among the younger generation who, in many ways, seem more open to receive than their elders".

* * * * * * * *

On my last visit to the Knapp in 1942, I was wearing the bell-bottomed trousers as an ordinary seaman. I forget where I was being sent, but it seemed to be an occasion for farewells. Dr. Nicoll went to his bookcase and pulled out a pleasantly bound copy of Swedenborg's "Divine Love and Wisdom", then, writing my name in it and his initials, thrust it into my hand. It has remained a treasured possession although I have never managed to read it from cover to cover. I find it easy to reach saturation point with that author, but Dr. Nicoll was wont to quote from him frequently.

Otherwise I have to rely on the memories of others in writing about the Birdlip era. There was one event in which my wife was involved, illustrative of the demands made on the staunch women who had to fend for themselves in the absence of their menfolk.

The hills of Birdlip were deep in drifting snow when an exhausted and relatively elderly "Dorothy" arrived at the Knapp saying that the car she had been driving was firmly embedded in a snowdrift some distance away. After enquiries as to how she had left the car, two other Dorothys were sent out to find the car, extinguish the lights and drain off the radiator. They carried a torch and appropriate spanners. It is true that Dr. Nicoll preferred women to be feminine, but not helplessly feminine. In wartime they should be able to wire electric plugs, mend fuses and effect other domestic repairs when necessary. On the respective roles of men and women, I recall an earlier remark at Tyeponds when we were boarding our cars to go home. Dr. Nicoll noted that a number of women occupied the driving seats in their cars. "I think times were better when the man climbed into the saddle with his woman behind him, and when they reached Hatfield forest, he would loosen his sword in its scabbard in order to deal with any robbers". Conditions change with time, however, and it may be that both sexes have to widen the scope of their activity, but as between a man and a women, there is a complementary difference in their roles which should not be blurred.

CHAPTER 7

Quaremead

After the war the Nicolls moved to the village of Ugley, Essex, and rented a house which was renamed "Quaremead". In the language of estate agents it was described as either "A desirable gentleman's residence" or "A gentleman's desirable residence", either description justly summing up the character of the house. It seemed ill-suited to Dr. Nicoll's being and, I think, nobody was sorry when the "Ugley" period came to an end.

Being in the process of demobilisation, picking up the threads of civilian life again and moving to a new home, my wife and I did not visit Ugley very often. Although I was aware that the Work was not designed to make us feel comfortable, I felt out of step with what went on there. Particularly I remember an evening in the local pub which was close to the entrance to the drive belonging to Quaremead. I was subjected to a review of my personal shortcomings. It seemed endless and loud enough for all the "locals" to hear. Had I had foreknowledge of a conversation to come much later, I should perhaps not have felt so bad about it. This was when I was responsible for a sub-group of my own and was told, "Yes. It is permissible to 'hit' people provided that at the moment of hitting you love that person more than you hate him. It must *never* be a mechanical reaction. Also, never hit a person that is not worth hitting. You hit with one hand and support with the other". It goes without saying that these provisos prohibited me from taking what I deduced must be "conscious" action. Another condition in the same context was, "you should never point out a person's 'Chief Feature', or indeed any other predominant feature of that person's False Personality until he is on the verge of seeing it for himself. Such disclosure could set him back years in his private work as he would justify and explain it away, thus forming dense scar tissue over the wound".

Again I feel it necessary to explain Work terms, in this instance "Chief Feature" and "False Personality".

We are born as Essence, that which *is*, from the Latin esse, to be. In the course of growing up Essence acquires around it from parents, education, teachers, hero-worship and imitation, material in the form of borrowed thoughts, feelings, opinions and habits, which, to the extent that it is useful, should be food for the growing being. All this is the stuff of Personality. Essence should learn from external life and for a few years it does. Then gradually a change takes place when Essence loses its sense of identity in what is relatively real and the child's feeling of itself passes into a strange amalgam of the acquired material of Personality. Persona were originally the masks which actors held before their faces and were appropriate to the parts they played. In the phenomenon of Personality and Essence it seems as though the actor forgets that he is wearing a mask and playing a part so that the mask and the part wear him. A man's feeling passes into his acquired wealth, fame, academic distinction, medal ribbons and attainments. He no longer wears his psychological clothes. They wear him. He is fundamentally no longer a "MAN without inverted commas", as Gurdjieff would say. Thence his task is to remember his royal descent, as in the parable of the Hymn of the Robe of Glory, and find his way home.

The substance of "*False* Personality" is not even potentially useful since it arises from self-love and conceit and it is in this that ordinary man can most easily be wounded. It is his imagination about himself which will fight for its life when threatened by a moment of sincere self-observation. In pathological cases suicide is possible if this bubble be pricked. A stock illustration will serve to show the difference between "Personality" and "False Personality".

A man may know quietly and confidently that he is a good shoe-maker. He cannot be hurt in this knowledge. If, however, he thinks that he is the best in Jermyn Street he may be put out when another is proved to be better. A slander action may be his last resort. More graphic examples may be found in the world of the arts.

Chief Feature is the core, the main characteristic, of False Personality and we manifest it in everything we do. No words can precisely define a man's Chief Feature, but a good cartoonist may sometimes come close to catching it.

My feelings may be very subjective, but the "discomfort" at Quaremead did not seem to be productive in the same way that previous "discomfort" had been. In "Work" surroundings it seems that there must always be a degree of muddle and friction which, if used, can lead to growth of understanding, whereas conditions of "Sweetness and Light" in excess may lead to sleep with sweet dreams. It is better to have a continuing question, and open-ended search, than a neatly organised regime with neatly typed notices on a notice board. Sweet, in another sense, are the uses of adversity, as Shakespeare wrote. Yes, but only if consciously and willingly used as a step towards self-knowledge.

Gurdjieff says, "We are here only to contend with ourselves. So thank others who provide you with the opportunity for doing so".

I am fairly certain that the Nicolls were not sorry to move on. Harking back to Ecclesiastes, could it be that they were mistaken in the choice of Quaremead? Was it the time and place? Dr. Nicoll was very sensitive to the appropriateness of time and place for different manifestations. He would start an activity and stop it immediately if he felt that it did not fit the situation. At every moment, in every circumstance, a limited number of law-conformable possibilities exist. The task was to allow the best to be fulfilled. What in us acted as pilot? Intellect, feeling, instinct or intuition? Plato uses the word "inspiration" in the meaning of a direct connection with the Gods. The Work uses the word "Consciousness", by derivation, "Knowing together", exactly in that sense that is with every centre*, every faculty inner and outer, with the whole being.

* * * * * * *

**Centres.* The "Work" gives a diagram of Man as a three-storey factory with Intellectual Centre in the top storey, Emotional Centre in the middle storey and Moving Centre in the lowest storey. Physically the head, thorax and abdomen correspond. A man thinks with his Intellectual Centre, feels with his Emotional Centre and moves his limbs and body with his Moving Centre. Later Instinctive Centre and Sex Centre are added to the lowest compartment in the diagram. Instinctive Centre attends to the inner working of the physical organism, digestion, breathing, circulation, waste rejection and many other functions.

Later still Higher Intellectual Centre and Higher Emotional Centre are included in the appropriate compartments.

The general concept of Centres is developed in many directions and Centres are sub-divided. Connections between Centres, some useful and others useless, are indicated; but to begin with students are recommended to observe in themselves the working of Centres and to distinguish between a thought, a feeling and a movement. Instinctive Centre may be observed but preferably not interfered with. The working of the High Centres cannot be directly observed because, although they are present and probably working, we, in our customary state of sleep, cannot be conscious of this for the reason that the "Voltage", so to speak, that they conduct would be too great for the faulty wiring of our system to carry. Chaos needs first to be replaced with cosmos (order).

It is a general aim to become balanced between Centres and between inner and outer parts of Centres. For this we need to make objective to ourselves our lack of balance and to notice how we have acquired a tendency mechanically to have a centre of gravity in one department at the expense of being equally developed in the others. A "Moving type", for instance, when confronted with a task, will tend to say, "Give me the tools and I will get on with it". An "Instinctive type" will be swayed by the considerations of comfort, temperature, the next meal or refreshment, etc. "Emotional type" will like or dislike the task, or the people he is required to work with. "Intellectual type" will theorize, draw plans and pick up a spade only as the ultimate resort. He will theorize about diet instead of allowing Instinctive Centre to know better in its own legitimate way.

It cannot be over-emphasized, however, that no one aspect of the Work teaching can be understood finally without the others. And this applies to the cosmological as well as the psychological teaching.

What one knows is only a part of a limitless whole and was there before we knew it. We open to knowledge and understanding. Plato again, "all knowledge is recollection".

No words can communicate all understanding. There must be a universal language beyond words, possibly one that makes communication possible between all sentient beings.

CHAPTER 8

Great Amwell House

If there were doubts about Quaremead fulfilling the needs of time and purpose, there were none about Great Amwell House. This was a gracious building of ample proportions to suit Dr. Nicoll's design for the Work. The setting of the house in its own grounds was ideal and whilst we should not lose ourselves in grandeur, it gave something to our endeavours.

Here the Work began to assume a perceptible "Nicoll" character.

Some members became residents for longer or shorter periods, but most came down for weekends, sleeping in the "boys" or "girls" dormitories when all the available bedrooms were occupied. Others came for the day and some only for meetings. There was domestic work and maintenance to be done in the house and garden, but this did not seem to take a disproportionate amount of time or effort. There was an ample supply of young and able bodies in the growing Group to cope with physical tasks. Some of the older hands who remembered the days at Tyeponds may have regretted the absence of the demands created by the building at that time and felt that the young were "having it too easy". At any rate they had the satisfaction of romancing about the days when work was work, lighting was by paraffin lamps and Elsan closets needed daily attention. The time for all that was over. This was a time for something other.

Many activities were started from time to time, acting, music, wood-carving, painting amongst them. Each had their season and were sometimes cut short. No activity was regarded as an end in itself. They were not intended to make the adept more adept. They were intended to open new ground which otherwise would lie fallow in people who would perhaps have neglected the experience, say, of painting or making music for the remainder of their lives; in short, to be more balanced in their experience and between their various centres. This opened doors. If real talent was discovered the individual could pursue it elsewhere, but this belonged to the category of "providing conditions". Once when we were singing Gilbert and Sullivan choruses with a strong professional soprano voice in our midst, Dr. Nicoll came storming in from his room and stopped us immediately, saying "No. It is not about this!" He gave no explanation. We had to divine what "this" might be.

Meetings were held on both Saturday and Sunday each weekend. Dr Nicoll was usually in the chair with a man beside him. The questions and answers were usually based upon a "Commentary" written during the week. These meetings were the focal point of the weekend, often attracting people who were neither "residents" nor "weekenders". The same papers were available for the sub-groups to discuss during the week, although, where this group consisted mainly of newcomers to Work ideas, the sub-group leader had the task of presenting the ideas, both psychological and cosmological, in as pure a form as he could, before opening his meetings for wider discussion.

The Group and the satellite sub-groups were growing rapidly at this time. Men and women were returning from wartime activities and many were searching for meaning after the insanity of war, so that more and more authority had to be delegated to older pupils to conduct sub-groups. These were held mostly in and around London. Until new people had received a grounding in the ideas, formulations and diagrams, lasting usually for several months, they were not introduced to Great Amwell House. By this time they were expected to have shown a genuine interest in the ideas of the Work and a desire to engage more fully in the various aspects of the teaching. This was not always neat and tidy for the sub-groups tended to form their own nuclei and their members continued going to sub-group meetings as well as to Amwell. However the sub-group leaders were discouraged from speaking of "my sub-group" in proprietorial terms.

Sub-group leaders were usually senior pupils—not so much in years as in Work experience—who had been instructed to start a sub-group or to take one over that already existed. Such appointments were always to be regarded as temporary and probationary and cancellation was not to be regarded as a sign of failure. Sometimes a pupil would ask for permission to start a group on these terms. Dr. Nicoll was heard to say on one such occasion, "X has asked for a sub-group, but he is not ready for it.

But then no man is ever ready or fit to have a sub-group until he has had one." Presumably he has to be given responsibility and to grow capable of bearing it in arrears.

In my own case, my sub-group somehow attracted a number of older men and women who had been left without a leader when Mr. Ouspensky died. These obviously needed accelerated promotion to Amwell and Dr. Nicoll's direct influence, although, as I said, they continued as a sub-group. Some of them were material for leadership of sub-groups themselves in quite a short time.

Since new people were coming into the Group all the time, propounding the basic ideas become a circular process with no fixed starting point or termination. Generally we went through the process about three times. The "ideas" were never finally "dealt with" as in training for a professional examination, for they were living ideas and inexhaustible in meaning.

The sub-group meetings were reported by its members in turn and were subject to comment or correction by Dr. Nicoll if the leader went wildly wrong. The quality and accuracy of these reports varied enormously. It was painful to realise how completely one could be misunderstood and misreported and one would long to put things right in Dr. Nicoll's mind. However he could be trusted to make allowances for this peculiarity, having been through the same experience himself in his time with Ouspensky.

Just occasionally a report would be so good that it seemed better than anything the leader could possibly have said, probably because of condensation, or because of the greater understanding of the reporter. Here the danger was more insidious. How not to take the merit to oneself and how to allow the possibility that the listener understood more than the speaker of the substance of ideas.

I have already written of some of the guidance I was given in the art of taking meetings, but I shall add an extract from a letter that Dr. Nicoll wrote on receipt of the report of my first sub-group meeting.

> "It was all right, but I had the same difficulty in O's groups. You gave them too much; too anxious to explain what you understand instead of listening to what they do not understand. And sometimes 'I don't know. What do you

think?' Be more dignified, dress carefully, speak clearly in the name of the Work. You are not trying to persuade papa and mama."

A little later I reported that a member of the sub-group had complained that too frequently I started with "Dr. Nicoll said . . ." so that he felt obliged to accept what was said as ex cathedra and was not able to argue in pursuit of his question. I was told that the man was quite right and that I must speak from myself, from my understanding and sometimes as though I knew. This was better than quoting others or manifesting a spurious humility. "To speak as though you know is a kind of blasphemy, but provided that you know you blaspheme it may be forgiven you. There is a passage in the Apocrypha concerned with a misdemeanour on the Sabbath day. 'If you know what you do you are blessed. If you know not you are accursed and also a transgressor of the Law'".

There was an occasion at Amwell when in Dr. Nicoll's absence I had to take a large meeting. By all accounts it went quite well; but his subsequent comment to me was: "Yes. It was all right. NO. It was bloody awful!" Then he said quietly "Catch? You may just register that it was adequate, but you must not take success or people's congratulations to yourself. It does not belong to you".

Later I read in his diary a comment on another occasion. "Told Copley not to go on and on". We never stop learning.

From time to time we performed some of the first six of Gurdjieff's "Movements" known to us as the "Obligatories". These had been given to us in pre-war days by Mrs. Howarth with Mrs. Nott at the piano. The services of these ladies, pupils of Mr. Gurdjieff, had been lent to the Nicoll group but were promptly withdrawn when it was observed that notes were being made of both the movements and the music. This was against the rules. Some of us, who later joined the Gurdjieff Society, found that our aim should not have been to "Learn" the movements, but to learn to work on ourselves by means of the movements. In fact, if we did master a movement to the extent of being able to perform it mechanically, it would no longer be of any benefit to us. The demand for attention in all parts of our being was of prime importance. Sometimes a posture or a movement, never made in ordinary life and outside the scope of our habitual associations, would give us a new impression of ourselves and a sense of wonder. Different limbs were required to move in different tempos and sometimes, when the mental memory was overtaxed, the body had to be trusted to find its own tempo. Then the members of the class would move about the floor in relation to a design and to one another. The class was a whole. To a degree, we were one another.

Of course those who were destined to teach the movements themselves in due course, or to be included in a public demonstration, were obliged to master the movements with accuracy; but then they would have extra and greater responsibilities later on. A teacher should be able to conduct the very spirit of the movements, the essence, the distilled inner meaning.

They were not drill or gymnastics and the "Obligatories" were a small part of a much greater whole.

The "Movements" or "Sacred Dances" were gathered by Gurdjieff in his search for truth amongst wise men and esoteric schools in the Middle East and Central Asia.

Some of the Sacred Dances have been recorded in films directed by Mme. Jeanne de Salzmann who, with her husband, were amongst Mr. Gurdjieff's earliest pupils. They are sometimes projected for the benefit of a wider public. Mme. de Salzmann, on Mr. Gurdjieff's death, was given the task of recording and co-ordinating, not only the Movements, but all aspects of the teaching for future generations.

Her continuing fulfilment of this task places her amongst the great ones of the Gurdjieff tradition. Perhaps a more able pen than this will one day provide the portrait of a vertical woman.

Dr. Nicoll must have undergone some training in the movements at the "Institute", but they did not occupy a large part in his transmission of the Work. In my opinion, we might have profited enormously had we continued with a gifted "movements" teacher who understood their meaning from the inside.

Nevertheless, what we did receive from Dr. and Mrs. Nicoll by way of teaching was unique and invaluable. Without intending criticism of, or comparison with any other teachers, I count myself more than fortunate in receiving the teaching in the way it was given to me by them. In any case they appeared in my life at a time that had all the significance of the now oft-quoted passage from Ecclesiastes, "a season for everything under the sun". Comparison therefore is meaningless. My contact with the teaching was in the design of things.

With the growing number of people surrounding Dr. and

Mrs. Nicoll, it was inevitable that pupils who had enjoyed close and frequent contact with their teachers were obliged to make room for younger men and women to move into closer orbit around the centre. Their time and force are limited. We had had our turn, and now we had to bear our own weight and to some extent the weight of newer people joining the Groups. I think that we understood the situation and had no feelings of jealousy. If we had experienced any "transference" and were not free from it then we were not sufficiently adult to have caught the message. We had never been allowed to feel ourselves "special" in any way and if we had been given responsibility for a period, we knew that this might well be transferred to another at any moment. He, or she, would be neither more nor less qualified to take it on, but would be given a task for some reason of his or her being. It was, for instance, more efficient to place money matters in the hands of an accountant, but it was sometimes necessary for an artist, musician or doctor to have to come down to earth and grapple with what is nowadays called the "nitty gritty". Earthy people, per contra, might have been landed with a responsibility equally at variance with their training in life.

I was once pushed into the meeting room at Amwell amongst a crowd of people and told, "Go and arrange the dance of the chromosomes". I had only a sketchy idea of what a chromosome was and certainly never knew that they danced, if indeed they do. So I quickly found an astute young man from my sub-group who happened to be at Amwell for the first time and asked what he knew of chromosomes and their dancing. Sagely he advised that it did not matter how they danced, but "arrange something, for others will be no wiser". The resultant muddle, and for me embarrassment, provided ideal "Work" conditions for all.

Although members of a sub-group would naturally prefer to take their personal problems to Dr. Nicoll, his time and force, as I have said, were limited so that sub-group leaders inevitably became involved in the private lives of some of their group. It was an interesting task to try to be objective about another person's difficulties in relationships and often other matters. The main effort of the sub-group leader was to listen and then, instead of telling the other person what to do, to open his eyes a little wider and to be more objective himself about his difficulties. If he could relax, widen his horizon and often allow a muddle to continue rather than tidy it all up, try to see the other person's point of view and take situations a little less seriously, he might find his own way out of the bog he had fallen into. We were sometimes given a specific exercise to try deliberately to adopt an opposite point of view and to think from that. Whatever opinions were held, they were to be held lightly, as between thumb and forefinger and taken up and put down with freedom. Psychological attitudes were defined as crystallised opinions with which we identify so that they become "truth" for the holder of the opinion. All our "attitudes" had to be observed and these crystals dissolved into a fluid solution of understanding. In this context the principle of relativity would be introduced. For us there was no absolute truth, but only relative truth, relative to all the surrounding conditions of time, place, psyche and context.

In spite of one's efforts to keep oneself out of the way there were occasions when one was tempted to imagine that one had helped another, particularly if one received effusive thanks. It was imperative to escape from this illusion. Help came from the Work and then from the other person's own efforts to see more objectively in the light of Work principles. If one gave way to the temptation to believe that one could "do" in this respect a lust for power could arise so that one no longer helped people for their sake but, instead, to feed one's own vanity. In the resisting of this temptation we had an example in Dr. Nicoll who kept himself clean from this kind of mud.

In dealing with personal problems Dr. Nicoll, because of his clear psychological vision, could go very directly to the root of the matter. On occasions he would be gentle and supportive and at other times very astringent and even coarse. Sometimes a convalescent returning to a group after an illness or surgical operation might anticipate a few kind words and advice to "take it easy" but instead would be treated to a terse comment about sacrificing self-pity and getting on with living. "Dining out" on hospital experiences was not a permissible luxury. It cannot be said that he employed any technique. He saw and listened on each occasion with each individual. Each such experience was new. There was no standard treatment. Your wordy question was one thing. Your essential need was another.

The limited numbers in the early days and the individual contact was so valuable that it was not easy to understand how we could progress without it. But it had always been his aim that we should more and more stand on our own feet and bear our own weight. I think Dr. Nicoll might have had a sense of failure if some, at least, of his older pupils had not given some evidence of this aim being on the way to fulfilment. Nevertheless even after some delegation through sub-groups, his force percolated through so that it was amazing how many people were held in awareness by Dr. Nicoll. Cohesion still continued.

More and more external organisation became necessary. The fiscal laws of the country had to be observed as well as the rules of the Charity Commissioners. We understood in a very material way what it means to be "under laws". The problem became, how to be free under laws.

Dr. Nicoll said to a few of us, "Numbers—how are you going to deal with them? Anyway that will be your problem not mine".

Various hints suggested that once our Groups reached a certain size and the form of their work became formalised and crystallised, even widely accepted as a religion, the esoteric content would become clouded over with the exoteric. It would be recorded in books for scholars to argue about. The real Work would have to find completely new forms of expression, although, for a time, there might remain a core of serious people in the organisation who remembered their aim and kept something alive.

In our recorded history Christianity in its origins was probably one of the most pure forms of esotericism. History records how soon men began to torture and slay each other in the name of what different sects came to regard as Christianity and in each case was far removed from what Christ taught. And yet with all the distortions, mistranslations and changing meaning of words, something can still be found in the Gospels of esoteric truth, this depending on the mind of the seeker and his ability to sift the grain from the chaff and to let the message fall on new ears.

Whether we liked it or not the Work had to change in its external manifestation. How to be versatile whilst retaining the spirit?

Although the Commentaries were the basis for discussion at the Amwell meetings, Dr. Nicoll's methods were Platonic in many respects. Question and answer was the form of the meetings, thus following the admonition of Socrates not to communicate instruction but to lead to the spontaneous discovery of truth by the questioner himself. Like Socrates, he was clear as to the borderline between truth that was teachable and that which was not, the recognition of the latter being akin to the "divine madness" which is not a human ailment but was defined as "An inspired departure from established usage". It was madness because what is seen in that state is not explicable in logical, sense-based terms. Following the principle that all knowledge is recollection, Socrates speaks of poets and artists as being copyists inasmuch as divine inspiration or intuition (both words are used) opens them to a sublime truth that already exists and which they do not create of themselves. This truth, in Socratic terms, is available to the "Soul". In the language of the Work, Essence might be a more appropriate word, since Gurdjieff gives a different connotation to the word "Soul" as meaning something that "man awakening" needs to create for himself from energy or substance conserved by non-identifying and conscious direction of attention. For "man asleep" Soul, if the word can be used at all, may be his point of greatest identification.

The prayer of Socrates at the conclusion of the dialogue with Phaedrus was echoed in many of Dr. Nicoll's talks and in his attitude to life.

> "Beloved Pan, and all ye other Gods that here abide, grant me to be beautiful in the inner man, and all I have of outer things to be at peace with those within. May I count only the wise man rich. And my store of gold be such as none but the good can bear."

The words "Soul", "Spirit" and "Inner Man" are for most of us philosophical abstractions which may have meaning when we are in a religious or philosophical mood. For Nicoll the meanings behind these words were permanent realities and became more and more the centre of gravity of his thinking and feeling.

He would point out that in the Great Octave of the Universe, or "Ray of Creation", the unmanifest stands higher in the scale of intelligence than the manifest. For example, an architect's design for a house is more "intelligent" than a finished house. More houses can be built from the same design, or can be modified to meet changing needs. The concept of "House" in general is wider still and includes every dwelling from bungalow to mansion. At the same time as a "descending" octave of manifestation proceeds from the "Do" of an architect's design, the builders fulfil an "ascending" octave. Relatively "unintelligent" bricks, mortar, timber and other materials are brought on to a site and then are assembled according to a design, so as to construct a "house" which is the high "Do" of an ascending octave and far more intelligent than the mere collection of raw materials, which as units constitute separate little "Do's" at the start of an octave of integration. The house is something more than the sum of its parts.

The general principle of Octaves or "Law of Seven" applies to everything in the universe as does the "Law of Three", so says the Work. Under Nicoll's guidance we studied them carefully and tried to detect their operation in various aspects of our daily lives. But the scope and grandeur of these concepts could not be encompassed in our notebooks or our formatory* minds alone. We needed, rather, to feel with our whole being that these principles encompassed us and, without pretending that we understood, to allow a continuing sense of mystery to permeate our thought; perhaps a touch of Plato's "divine madness", supra-logical thought or metanoia.

Books, including notebooks, have limited use. They may act as reminding factors sometimes to stir us in our sleep, but reading them may become a substitute for experience. Perhaps it was for this reason that Dr. Nicoll reserved the right to confiscate our notebooks and Gurdjieff so often derided "wiseacreing".

---

*Although the word "formatory" does not appear in the O.E.D., it is frequently found in the English translations of Gurdjieff's and particularly Ouspensky's writings. The meaning is "intellectual" in a dry-as-dust way and is used in a pejorative sense.

CHAPTER 9

Health

The substance of this chapter has not been included in the earlier chapter on medicine for the reason that what I am now describing are some of the views that Dr. Nicoll expressed long after the professionally medical period of his life had ended.

As I have already indicated Dr. Nicoll was interested in the "whole" man and the whole man in relation to his environment. If he placed particular emphasis on the "inner man" or physically unmanifest man, it was because he considered that the existence of the inner man was insufficiently recognized as a subject for objective study. This did not mean that the outer man could be neglected for, to refer back to the remark of the Zen priest quoted previously, inner order and outer order are necessary one for the other. Man lives in an ordered universe or Cosmos and is—or should be—a cosmos himself conforming to universal laws. That chaos exists from time to time and from place to place is undeniable; but it is relative. What appears as chaos on one level may have significance on another. A ploughshare passing through an ant hill probably constitutes a national disaster to the ants. Whilst a straight furrow appears as orderly farming to the ploughman.

As a part of the film of organic life, which is a transforming station of influences received from celestial bodies, man needs for his own existence good fresh food, clean air and fresh impressions through his senses. He needs to exercise all his functions in a balanced manner. Dietary fads and theories counted for little with Dr. Nicoll. A freely functioning and undistorted "Instinctive" Centre knew better than the theorists provided that a man had not lost the capacity for listening to Instinctive Centre. Peculiar forms of physical exercise, breathing control and so on, sometimes passing under the label of "Yoga" had to be regarded with suspicion. A genuine form of Yoga might not be suitable for Western Man even though an oriental might profit from it. One needed a real teacher, a universal man, with a wide understanding of the physiology and the psychology of all men. In "A New Model of the Universe", P. D. Ouspensky writes of the different forms of Yoga and his description of "Karma Yoga" makes it appear to be the most suitable for modern Western man. This combines the "Ways" of Fakir, Monk and Yogi in a certain sense, and, above all, is the "Way in the midst of Life" using life as it presents itself as a necessary medium for growth. In this way lies freedom for the King on his throne and for the prisoner in gaol.

Many illnesses arise from acquired bad habits of eating, drinking, breathing, posture, movement and tension, but above all from useless psychic habits of identifying, imagining, negative emotions, self-justifying, internal considering and habitual negative thinking.

All these are described in the "Work" books. Illness arises because man has lost the capacity to listen to what his different centres have to tell him, each in their own language. Consequently he does not combine with his environment or place in the external cosmos so as to receive the necessary forms of nourishment, nor to fulfil his proper functions in a law-conformable manner.

When our daughter was born it was the fashion to adopt a strict programme of feeding times, exercise, exposure to the sun and a-sepsis was so important that one almost had to wear a mask when approaching a child. Kissing, cuddling and other germ-transmitting habits were frowned upon. Dr. Nicoll's robust comment was that babies needed human love and warmth and damn the germs. For each body there was an antibody generally speaking and if a baby was kept germ free and antibody free, it "would not half catch a packet" when, inevitably, it was obliged to enter the germ-ridden world.

The Nicoll's own granddaughter was delivered in a nursing home close to where we were living and I remember Mrs. Nicoll's delight when she came across the matron unawares and found her cuddling the baby for the natural joy of doing so. The early impressions of the child were of great importance and would be so much better in these conditions than in the cold clinical surroundings that belonged to that era in maternity homes.

When he was living at Birdlip Dr. Nicoll took up walking long distances over the Cotswolds for the purpose, I believe, of weight reduction. This was, I think, a deviation from his principles for he thought that physical exercise and recreation were for the enjoyment of whatever you were doing while you were doing it and not with an attitude of grim determination to keep fit or improve the waistline. In a poem he tells of a boyhood deception when he satisfied his parents with a tale of a non-existent walk:

> "That's good", they said,
> "it will keep you fit".
> "Fit for what?" I wondered.

If one can observe oneself objectively and learn once again to listen to the various centres or systems, psychological and physical, so that a natural order can be re-established, many illnesses would fade away because strictly speaking they do not belong to us, being attracted not by what is essential in us, but by our acquired psychology. They might be called accidental. Suppose that you are day-dreaming when crossing the road, perhaps about a conversation with your employer that you are expecting to have—or have had, and walk under a bus, the resulting damage might well be termed psycho-somatic in origin. It could not have occurred if you had been present in your body and awake to sensory impressions. There is also the diminished resistance to disease resulting from chronic anxiety, fear, jealousy and so on. Not being a practised or fluent after-dinner speaker, I know from experience how absurdly upset my digestive system can become prior to standing up and how immediately the speech is finished I feel that I could now enjoy a good meal. Alas too late! This is a small example, but undeniable evidence of how stress inhibits good order and is typical of the disorders affecting modern western businessmen.

On the other hand diseases arise which appear not to be accidental but to have a cognitive quality. There is something to be learnt from them. Sometimes illness is necessary to quieten the noise of traffic in robust good health in order that one can hear something that otherwise would be missed. In high fever one can have a subtle glimpse of another kind of reality. This can even change one's direction in life.

My sister went to a tough North Country boarding school whose motto might have been—but was not—"Girls will be boys". In those first world war days they played hockey, lacrosse and cricket seriously, and my sister had ambitions to be selected for various teams. But illness, broken collar-bones, and the like, seemed to baulk her progress. Telling this to Dr. Nicoll years later, he remarked "Thank goodness something or somebody was looking after you. This 'games' stuff did not belong to you and you were saved from going down that road".

A young actress returned from a holiday in Italy with an attack of jaundice and whilst still on a regime of protein and no alcohol went to stay at Amwell for a few days. She writes, "When I arrived Dr. Nicoll insisted on my drinking a glass of Pernod. I told him this was not allowed. He gave me another. 'Would I die?' I wondered. 'Should I go back to bed?' No, I felt much better. 'You see', he said, 'one can go on being ill too long'."

Reverting to the interplay of the psychic and the somatic, Dr. Nicoll recounted the story of a doctor who contracted a disease in which he specialised. The illness had a prognosis with a well defined timetable and the doctor was delighted to have first hand experience and took an objective interest in his condition. The result, in some ways unfortunate, was that he recovered almost immedia ely as the usual prognosis was not followed. The inference was that an objective interest and a morbid identification can produce diametrically opposite results. In his last illness Dr. Nicoll himself made short clinical notes, recording the degree of haematuria, results of drugs taken and the signs (presumably not symptoms). There was nothing of hypochondria in this as he was getting up and taking meetings when he could, right up to the last few days of his life.

He told an amusing anecdote of Ouspensky telling a group that the contraction and dilation of the iris, according to the strength of the light, was managed by the Instinctive Centre automatically and could not be controlled at will through the mind, whereupon one member disagreed and proceeded to show that he could control his iris. He was told that, in fact, he cheated. He did not control his muscles by will but visualised light and darkness alternately. Importance was attached to the power of visualisation. In discussing Gurdjieff's parable of the Horse, Carriage and Driver we speculated upon the significance of the reins, that is the means by which the Driver (Intellectual Centre) communicated with the Horse (Emotional Centre) since neither spoke in the other's language. Dr. Nicoll felt that "visualisation" or controlled imagination (image-making) was something that the mind could do consciously and that the Emotional Centre could pick up. No one interpretation, however, was ever sufficient where parables were concerned as symbolism was multi-dimensional. He did confess an uncomfortable semi-belief that the "Black Magic" practice of making an image of an enemy in some plastic substance and sticking pins in it with thoughts of violence might have some validity. The practices of some primitive races would seem to corroborate. Meanwhile the "White" magic of Nicoll's visualisation of absent members of his Group in times of stress could be equally valid in a more progressive direction.

It may seem that we have strayed a long way from the subject of health, but from a "Nicoll" point of view health is resultant upon understanding and conforming with the "laws" or cosmic influences governing that level of the universe in which we live, "Understanding" rather than "Knowing-all-about", because recognition of the laws is as much a matter of feeling and sensation as of simply possessing intellectual knowledge. As I have said "illness" or temporary chaos may be intended by some sort of guardian angel sometimes to draw one's attention to the fact of one's straying from Law Conformity. From the point of view of an intelligence higher than our own, this apparent divergence may accord with a higher form of order which permits such warnings as a gift from above.

Dr. Nicoll had interesting comments to make about a substance or energy denoted as "Fa.96" in the Work terminology. The Work teaches that man has three foods, food we eat, air we breathe and impressions that we take in through all our senses, internal and external. Their relative importance can perhaps be measured by the fact that a man may live for days without food per mouth, minutes without air and practically not at all without impressions. Their digestion conforms to the Law of Seven (Octaves) and the Law of Three (Triads). Just how is described in the "Work" books. Ordinary food enters the digestive system as a substance with the density called H.768 as a "Do" in the food octave. This is transformed into a more liquid substance, Re.384 and then into a gas, Mi.192. Here the process of transformation comes to the place of constriction, or missing semi-tone, where it needs help from outside to proceed. This is provided by the shock of air coming into the lungs and the substance Fa.96 is produced. The first three substances are physically measurable and can be chemically analysed. But Fa.96 is something rarer than a gas and approaching a psychic energy. It is perceptible, but scarcely measurable. It has some relationship to muscle tone and radiant physical health. One definition was that "it makes you so tough that fleas don't bite you". Dr. Nicoll said that surgeons often had it in abundance as well as physiotherapists who can spare some for the benefit of patients. Without going into theories about antibodies, it seems that many immunities are carried along by Fa.96 and it can be quickly exhausted by negative emotions and other wrong, or non-law-conformable psychic functions. However Fa.96 should undergo further transformation into the higher energies of thought and emotion and eventually sex energy. If too much is retained as 96, there seems to be a kind of "constipation" in which robust health leads to insensitivity to finer experience. More often, as was reported in a note of a conversation (23.5.48) "The demons eat Fa.96, it's Mars Bars to them". The demons being negative emotions and identifying.

CHAPTER 10

The External World

Whilst Dr. Nicoll dwelt constantly on the psychological, spiritual and suprasensory capacities of man, he was also a man of the earth and accorded full respect to those who coped efficiently and enjoyably with the material side of life. He could learn from the experts in all trades, crafts and professions. When he conversed with admirals, high ranking soldiers or any others who had risen high in their respective callings, he was genuinely interested in what they had to say and, because of this, they reciprocally found him interesting. Without being an expert himself, he had the ability to find his way to the centre of gravity of what was being discussed and often had pertinent comments to make. Equally he could engage with country craftsmen in a similar fashion. Once, during my temporary naval career, he questioned me on the difference between barques and barquentines, brigs and brigantines. He was reading C. S. Forrester's "Hornblower" stories at the time. When I confessed my igorance, beyond knowing that they were sailing vessels with different rigging, I was unbraided, "You are living amongst all this wonderful stuff of ships, boats and rigging, and you don't know. You pass too much in faeces without assimilating much that you could extract from this rich source of the food of impressions".

Nicoll's pupils were encouraged to keep their feet on the ground and never to feel superior to life nor to "Life" people who were not "in the Work". At the same time, we were expected to be a little more than "adequate" in any tasks that we undertook. I was told, "Try to do what you do with a degree of flair. You cannot afford to be average". Strangely I was told the same thing by a senior naval officer in almost the same words, but in a more limited context.

All this stemmed from the principle that the Work was not an escape from life, but, on the contrary, life provides the raw material for work. We were required to recognize and allow the fulfilment of our potentials in all respects of our lives. There should be, with the "Philosopher's Stone" of the Work, a transmutation of base metal into gold. We were reminded that the Work was sometimes called "The Way of Sly Man". In the Gospels Christ remarked that "The children of this world are, in their generation, wiser than the children of light". The children of light could and should learn from the children of the Earth. Likewise the disciples were told to be wise as serpents and harmless as doves. There is also, I believe, a Tibetan saying to the effect that he who knows how to go about it could live comfortably in Hell. The children of light having acquired wisdom, slyness or cleverness should be able to use it without being used by it.

We had in our midst a lady who was the wife of an equerry to a royal prince. She moved socially in circles remote from the experiences of most of us. With never failing cheerfulness, generosity and goodwill she took many of us, who were rough diamonds to say the least, to be immersed for a spell in the kind of world in which she moved. Here we had the opportunity to learn how to walk and talk with princes or with dustmen with some degree of freedom and without obsequiousness on the one hand or patronage on the other and finding all men and women interesting. Good manners, after all, are something more than a facade. I doubt whether she ever realised how well she served Dr. Nicoll and his Work in this and other ways. She might have been numbered amongst those who asked, "When saw we thee a stranger and took thee in or as hungered and fed thee, or athirst and gave thee drink?" She did what she did naturally, generously and with no idea of "doing good".

In the field of "Lifemanship" I owe another debt to an announcer and news-reader on the old BBC Light Programme who took me in hand when I had been sharply criticised for my poor reading aloud of the Commentaries. With endless patience and care he showed me how to phrase a script in readable sections, what to emphasize and throw away, at the same time maintaining a sort of legato line and above all to avoid the English habit of dropping my voice at the end of phrases and sentences. Finally he reminded me that an audience can only understand what you read after you have you spoken it. Therefore the reader must take responsibility for deciding where the meaning lies. The listener has to digest one sentence while listening to the next and needs every possible consideration from the reader in this difficult task.

I cannot leave this subject of respect for life and people in life without quoting Mrs. Nicoll who, speaking of the "Ways" said, "Remember there are other ways than the Fourth Way which we study. There is the "Way of Good Householder". That is an ordinary man or woman who does the decent thing rather than the indecent, obeys the laws of the land and social conventions, not devoutly believing in either but realising the chaos that would ensue from neglecting them. This way is a slow way, but even so, you may find a Good Householder ahead of you in understanding and being".

CHAPTER 11

The Summing Up

What Dr. Nicoll said and wrote was of great importance. What he was and how he manifested his being was of greater importance. It must surely have been the same with Gurdjieff since the impression I have from those who currently carry on the Gurdjieff teaching is that although words, diagrams, movements and other exercises are indispensable vehicles, the spirit of the Work requires the "Being" of its teachers to give them the vibrations of life.

Esoteric means "Hidden", "Secret", "available to those who have ears to hear", so that once something has been expressed in speech or writing it has to some extent come out into the open in a form of manifestation that cannot exactly fit it. The spoken word can perhaps retain more of the esoteric than the written word for something is transmitted in the manner of telling. With the written word it is necessary to "read between the lines". What is *not* said also has significance. In a still life art class we were told not only to observe the solid objects but also the spaces in between. Thomas a Kempis speaks of the soul as "She" and "Her". Jung teaches the "anima" of men and the "animus" of women, i.e. the unmanifest complements in each case. Thomas a Kempis writes of the prophets, "Beautifully do they speak but if Thou be silent, they kindle, not the heart. They give the letter, but Thou dost disclose the spirit. They announce the mysteries but Thou dost unlock their secret meaning . . . Speak Lord, for thy servant hears thee, for Thou has the words of eternal life". The same writer says "Happy is the man whom truth teaches by itself, not by figures and passing words but as it is in itself".

So between the lines, between the world manifest to the senses and an internal world, a teacher of esoteric truth tries to express that which is almost inexpressible. At best he will only be heard by those whose ears are open to hear and perhaps the teacher's greatest task is to create conditions in which a limited number of potential listeners can begin to open their ears by their own deliberate conscious effort. To quote again Dr. Nicoll's advice to me, "You are not trying to persuade papa and mama". If you cannot persuade you certainly cannot compel people to hear.

Towards the end of his life Dr. Nicoll had a dream about a difficult-to-cross ditch to which he attached considerable importance. It is described in a short addition to "The Mark" under the heading of "The New Will". Because it seems to summarise his life of endeavour it is reproduced here:-

"Someone pushes me up a grass slope. There is a ditch. It is not wide but difficult to cross. The difficult-to-cross ditch at the top of the slope is full of the bones of prehistoric animals—the remains of violent things, of beasts of prey, of monsters, of snakes. They go far down into the abyss. There is a plank to cross by, but the air seems full of restraining power, like the invisible influence of some powerful magnet; and this, with the fear of crossing this depth—although the width is not great—holds one back. I cannot say for how long for there is no ordinary time in all this. Then I find myself across—ON THE OTHER SIDE. What wonderful vision do I now behold? I see someone teaching or drilling some recruits. That is all. At first sight there seems nothing marvellous. He smiles. He indicates somehow that he does not expect to get any results from what he is doing. He does not seem to mind. He does not show any signs of impatience when they are rude to him. The lesson is nearly over, but this will not make any difference to him. It is as if he said, "Well, this has to be done. One cannot expect much. One must give them help, though they don't want it". It is his invulnerableness that strikes me. He is not hurt or angered by their sneers or lack of discipline. He has some curious power but hardly uses it. I pass on marvelling that he could do it. I could not take on such a thankless task. Eventually I come to a place, perhaps a shop, where boats are stored. Beyond is the sea.

When I wake I think of this man. To do what he is doing is so utterly contrary to anything I would do. I would need a new will to do it.

It would mean I would have to go in a direction I never went in. I thought much about this direction. How could I define it to myself? I would have been violent to those recruits. Yes. That was it. He showed no violence. He had not a will of violence. He seemed purified from all violence. This was the secret. That was the source of the curious power I detected in him. A MAN

WITHOUT VIOLENCE. And then I reflected that to reach him I had had to get across the other side of the deep gulf full of the bones of prehistoric beasts, full of the remains of violent creatures. This had been done for me somehow and I found myself on the border of another country, at the edge of it only, but beyond the prehistoric beasts. Here this non-violent man lived and taught. It was the country of the non-violent, where recruits were being taught. They seemed an indifferent lot but perhaps they represented people who could learn something eventually.

He had nearly finished his lesson. Beyond was the sea and there were boats stored near it. No doubt, when he had finished the course he was going on somewhere, beyond the land. As for me, I had been given only a glance into the meaning of a new will—a will not based on violence or having your own way. I repeat—only a glance. For I knew I had not, save in spirit, really crossed that deep gulf yet, filled with the bones of the violent past and left it behind finally. There were no recruits for me—or were the recruits different "I"s in myself that he was trying to teach? Certainly none of the waiting boats was mine. But from this glance I know more practically what going in a new direction is and what a new will purified from violence means. I know also that the possibilities of following this new will and new direction lie *in every moment of one's life*—and I forget".

After meeting Gurdjieff and Ouspensky, therapy was not the central aim of Dr. Nicoll's endeavour. Good health and normal functioning might reasonably be expected from a man's efforts to awaken, but as by-products only. He tried to distil and transmit the very essence of the "Work" with as little adulteration as possible, hence his insistence that his "Commentaries" were not the Work itself. Speaking of essence in a more material way, Dr. Nicoll once remarked that a grain of musk could scent a cathedral, not just for hours but for years. The essence of truth has the same quality. Two or three words from various parts of the Bible or a moment of real work live in eternity, although thay may be screened away in periods of passing time. Philosophers, psychologists and other commentators may write volumes about one grain of truth. Their labours are not entirely valueless, but they dilute. "Beautifully do they speak but they do not kindle the heart", to requote Thomas a Kempis. "They give the letter".

A moment in which Dr. Nicoll tried to show you something

of yourself and asked "Catch?" contained a grain of musk if, in fact, you did catch. Such is vertical truth, existing in eternity, sometimes piercing the clouds to illuminate a moment in time and accessible by a special effort of remembering.

POSTSCRIPT

St. John's Gospel opens, "In the beginning was the Word (Logos) and the Word was with God and the Word was God". In verse 14 we read, "And the Word was made flesh".

In this context the Greek "Logos" means something much more fundamental than "Word". "The essence of all meaning" might be a more adequate translation or "Signatura Rerum", as Boehme entitled his book. "Being made flesh" could bear more than one interpretation, "Flesh" in the body of Jesus Christ certainly, but also in the expression or manifestation of His teaching. It would seem that God as pure meaning cannot reach humanity unless it is given form in one way or another and "giving form" fulfils a necessary law.

Perhaps this is what esotericism is all about. But while expression clothes the spirit, it is not the spirit in itself. To some extent there is a dilution of spirit and the expression is mortal. It has a limited life span. The spirit is immortal. The expression also becomes subject to misunderstanding and misinterpretation in the communication of ordinary men and women. This mortality appears to conform to "Laws".

G. I. Gurdjieff, P. D. Ouspensky and Maurice Nicoll, each according to his capacity and his level of being, have been, and are, in the dimension of eternity, among the trustees or guardians of the "Logos", for their concern was to ensure that something of the spirit should reach mankind by the adroit use of the means of expression available to each in his own idiom. Knowing the laws, they understood that the vehicles used for conveyance of meaning were subject to wear and tear and obsolescence. But, hopefully, the essential substance conveyed would reach a few men and women for profitable employment, not only in their own development but by percolation for the benefit of all mankind.